The Weapons of W
to have in his or her "library arsenal." I can't stress enough how important this book is for the Christian wanting to be more prepared to be a strong worker for Christ. I truly believe that if you read this book prayerfully, no matter where you were on your Christian journey before, by the end of the book you will have moved closer to Christ and more equipped for victorious living.

—Edward B. Stokes
Pastor (Retired)
United Methodist Church, Bath, NC

Patrick Bucksot has written an excellent book The Weapons of Our Warfare. He gives a relevant presentation on the subject with clarity and the spirit of revelation. He shares how we can have complete victory and mastery over Satan. This book is a "Must Read" for the Body of Christ. I am convinced it will transform your life.

—Rev. Jessie H. Blalock
Senior Pastor
Word of Life International Church, Tarboro, NC

The Weapons of our Warfare is a scripturally based book that will encourage and challenge any Christian. Patrick takes you through a systematic look at our spiritual weapons that are available for the advancement of our Lord's Kingdom. A great study aid for all who wish a deeper understanding of the battle that is before us and how we can overcome in the name of Jesus.

—Dr. Steve Simpson
Pastor, River Bend Baptist Church
New Bern, NC

THE WEAPONS
of our
WARFARE

Becky,

Thank you for your Kingdom work. Praying this book inspires you to greatness in God!

Fight the Good Fight of Faith

1 Tim 6:12

Patrick Busby

Patrick A. Bucksot

THE WEAPONS
of our
WARFARE

God's Arsenal
for Victorious Living

TATE PUBLISHING
AND **ENTERPRISES**, LLC

Published by Tate Publishing & Enterprises, LLC
127 E. Trade Center Terrace | Mustang, Oklahoma 73064 USA
1.888.361.9473 | www.tatepublishing.com

Tate Publishing is committed to excellence in the publishing industry. The company reflects the philosophy established by the founders, based on Psalm 68:11,
"The Lord gave the word and great was the company of those who published it."

Book design copyright © 2012 by Tate Publishing, LLC. All rights reserved.
Cover design by Kristen Verser
Interior design by Sarah Kirchen

Published in the United States of America

ISBN: 978-1-61862-825-1
Religion / Biblical Studies / General
12.05.08

DEDICATION

Although there are many people who have touched my life in Christ, this book is dedicated to three special men who played a part in my maturing as a Christian. Pastor Owen Lupton, Pastor Blaney Rowe, and Pastor Ron Estes have, in their own calling of the Lord, ministered to me with the Word of God. They each gave me opportunities to develop in ministry and grow in my calling. I want to extend my gratitude to them for their obedience to the Father and pouring so much into my life.

This book is also dedicated to the memory of
April Renee Torres.

April 2, 1978 – August 25, 2008

It was through her tragic death that God had led me to pray for her family and the man who murdered April. The Lord revealed Himself in a powerful way when I told Him that He would have to give me the strength to love and forgive the murderer of one of my children. He said that love and forgiveness only come from Him and that they were two of His weapons of warfare written about in 2 Corinthians 10:4. Although April's death was tragic, the Lord is using it to minister the truth about how we can live a life of complete victory in Christ. I pray that anyone who knew April knows that she has not died in vain, and anyone who is touched by the contents of this book is a part of the legacy of her memory.

ACKNOWLEDGEMENTS

I wish to thank the Lord for His love, compassion, and calling. Without Him I could not have written this book. His love and grace over me is, without question, the reason my life is still together. I am thankful to my wonderful bride for giving me the time to write. Her support is unwavering. Her love is unmatched. And her devotion to the Lord is like nothing I have ever witnessed. I also want to thank my children, Marissa and David. I love you both more than you'll ever know. And lastly, I want to thank the readers of the Breath of God International Outreach newsletter from which this book was born. Your prayers and faithful encouragement to me and my writing has been priceless. God bless you all.

TABLE OF CONTENTS

FOREWORD

Turning people toward complete dependency on Christ is the goal of discipleship. The true beauty of God's unchanging grace and mercy are revealed through the essence of His eternal expression, which is His Word. God's Word is not just a book called "The Bible." God's Words are Spirit and they are life. They are more than words on a page; they are divinely empowered life giving forces that God has established from eternity past, present and future for the benefit of man.

The greatest purpose of man is to discover who he is created to be. Discovering purpose is made possible through the endless revelation of God's immense faithfulness to His Word. God's Word craftily calculates the innate need man has to change his current condition. Because of sin, man is separated from God and has come short of the glory of God. Through faith in the blood of Jesus Christ man has access to a living and real intimate relationship with God.

It is because of Christ that those who have faith in Him have been rescued from the kingdom of darkness and brought into the kingdom of the Son that God loves. The kingdom of the Son of God is an eternal kingdom that shall never pass away or be destroyed. He has established His kingdom with judgment and justice and will reign for now and for evermore. It is God's good pleasure to give you this kingdom.

Knowing and understanding these kingdom truths about God is why I am so excited about Patrick's book, Weapons of Our Warfare. Patrick has released many valuable tools to equip people who desire to move forward from a life of follower-ship to a life of discipleship. Weapons of Our Warfare will equip you on how to go above and beyond just attending church. It will prepare you to become the church.

Just as every solider needs basic training in order to be more effectively prepared for the battles they will encounter in life, every believer needs basic training in God's eternal principle to stand strong in their faith in Christ. Weapons of Our Warfare is a basic training manual drawn from the life experiences of Patrick Bucksot. I believe that you have not stumbled upon this book aimlessly. Perhaps you will find in these pages some basic answers to help you become a more committed disciple of the Lord Jesus Christ.

—Dr. Andrew Bucksot
Multi-Cultural Missions
Atlanta, Georgia

INTRODUCTION

Throughout the Word of God there have been epic battles recorded about the nation of Israel. Israel suffered many defeats but also had many great victories. The notable thing about their defeats is that they came in the wake of disobedience to God. Just prior to their defeats they would have walked away from the Lord. When they began to worship idols, their next battle ended in defeat. Defeat came when they allowed other gods into their worship and began to make rituals for them. Israel also saw defeat when they became complacent about God. When they became comfortable in their status, they believed that since things were going well they did not need God.

We might ask ourselves why God allowed so many defeats of the Israelite nation, given the fact the He is supposed to be loving and merciful. That is a fair question, but we have to look at the incredible victories that Israel had in order to find the answers. In the greatest battles of the nation of Israel, they defeated armies that were bigger, faster, and stronger. They defeated their enemies with great power, but it was not at their doing. These military achievements could only come at the hand of God. And I believe that this is best explained in Judges chapters six and seven. In chapter six, God called Gideon to save Israel. Gideon was surprised at this because his family was poor and he was the smallest of his father's house. Just like us, Gideon was looking at the outward appearance, but God had called him a "mighty man of valor."

In chapter seven, after Gideon had prepared his army, God told him that his army was too big. God told him that he needed to let everyone who was afraid to go home. Amazingly, twenty-two thousand people left the camp. Gideon, now left with 10,300 men, was told again that his army was still too big. He was told this because God did not want Israel to rest in their own power and might. God knew that if He let them go into battle at full strength, they would have been confident in themselves and not in the power of God. God put Gideon's army through another test, and Gideon was left with just three hundred men after another ten thousand left the camp. Gideon's army, now just three hundred strong, was going to fight the might army of the Midianites. Gideon, with his small army and the strength of the hand of God, defeated the Midianites.

Another epic battle was when Joshua led Israel to victory over Jericho. Jericho had a mighty army, but their strength came in the form of an impenetrable wall around their city. Joshua could have had an army of millions, but the wall was their barrier to victory. In other words, there was nothing within human strength and understanding that Israel could have done to destroy the city of Jericho. Well beyond human understanding, God commanded Joshua to have his army march around the city once each day and on the seventh day, seven times. And while marching, they were to remain completely silent; that, in and of itself, seemed impossible. The only sound that God allowed them to make was at the end of the seventh march on the seventh day. I am certain that we would have given up long before the time came for a shout. However, the army of Israel was obedient to the Word of God. When they shouted, the mighty walls of Jericho came down, and so did its city. The mind of man could not have conceived this scheme or built any weapons to do what God did on that day.

Now we go to one of the greatest battles of all: David and Goliath. In boxing terms, the tail of the tape had Goliath standing at around nine feet, nine inches tall with just one portion of his armor weighing in at 125 pounds. The head of his spear weighed around fifteen pounds so his spear must have been about the size of a small tree. David, on the other hand, may have been between five feet, six inches to five feet, nine inches tall and was no obvious match to Goliath. When King Saul tried to give David his own armor, David refused because it was not made for him, it was too big for him, and he did not have time to test it. Instead, he went with what he was comfortable using—a sling and a stone. It was this weapon that David used to protect his father's sheep, and he was very skilled in its use. However, he went with more than a sling and a few stones. David was armed with his complete confidence in the Lord. David proclaimed that God had delivered the bear and the lion into his hand, and Goliath would also be delivered into his hands. I personally believe that if David and Goliath ended up in a wrestling match Goliath would have been killed by David.

In each of these battles, what seemed impossible in the eyes of man was possible with God. And with each victory came a confidence in the Lord again. The nation of Israel saw the mighty hand of God, turned from their wicked ways, and surrendered their obedience to Him. Let it be said here that God never left Israel. It was the nation of Israel who left Him.

So how does this apply in our lives today and our weapons of warfare? One simple word can answer that question: everything. We fight in spiritual battles every day. We win some and we lose some. We can't seem to live a life of complete victory over our enemy. It almost feels like we stay in some form of bondage or another. I believe that this is true because we don't really understand where our battles begin. I am talking about the war that rages between our renewed spirit and our flesh. While we wrestle with the flesh, we cannot war against it with fleshly things, because our spirit man can only use weapons from a spiritual source. Our source for our spiritual weapons comes from the armory of God. This armory, or weapons depot, is stocked with a great many weapons that are designed to bring us victory in our lives and for the kingdom of God. Second Corinthians 10:3-4 says, "For though we walk in the flesh, we do not war according to the flesh. For the weapons of our warfare are not carnal but mighty through God for the pulling down of strongholds."

If we were to try to win a battle over our flesh with fleshly things, it would be like fighting a house fire with fire. The house would quickly be consumed because the correct tool to fight the fire was kept away from the battle. Now I know that the forestry service will perform controlled burns, so, in a way, we could say that they fight fire with fire. That is only partly true. They have controlled burns to keep the forest from being completely consumed if a large fire was started. I guess you could say that we need to allow the Holy Spirit into our lives to perform controlled burns to get rid of the small underbrush of sin that, if they go unchecked, will become major problems down the road.

The weapons of God are not carnal or formed by the hands of man, so we can't take any credit for our victories. In the battles of Joshua and Jericho, Gideon and the Midianites, and David and Goliath, God stacked the military deck against the enemies of Israel with His mighty hand. Israel could not take any glory for their victories because God made sure that the battles would require a miracle to win. He does the same thing in our lives. When we have a battle before us, like needing to forgive someone who has wronged us, God supplies our weapon for victory. Why? Because we can't forgive from the flesh. Our flesh man will only desire revenge.

As you read this book, I believe that God will open your heart to receive Him as the one who provides victory for your life. Now, you may not agree with everything that I write, and that's okay. My prayer is that God reveals Himself to you in a more powerful way and you will desire to get into His Word and His presence. I also pray that if you don't know Jesus as your Lord and Savior, this book will begin your journey into the Word of God. At the end of this book, there will be an opportunity for you to give your heart to Jesus.

THE WORD OF GOD

When God saved us, He had big plans for our lives. He gave each one of us spiritual gifts and a special calling to enhance His kingdom. He also gave us liberty from sin. With such freedom comes great responsibility. We still have an adversary who is trying to derail everything that we believe and understand about God. He will do anything to trip us up and make us look foolish before each other and the world. We are in a constant battle between our renewed spirit and our old, carnal nature. The only true help for us comes from the Lord. It's true that we can and should encourage one another in the faith, but only God can deliver us from temptation and sin.

Second Corinthians 10:4 says, "The weapons of our warfare are not carnal, but mighty through God to the pulling down of strongholds." We have been given particular weapons of warfare to do battle against the devil and bring our flesh into subjection to the Spirit of God. Our spiritual weapons, unlike the military weapons of a nation, can only be used to build up the kingdom of God, His children, and draw us closer to Him. If we do anything that hinders the growth of God's kingdom or hurt the body of Christ, we are using the tools and weaponry of our old flesh.

The weapons of the flesh can only tear down and destroy. We do have a complete arsenal of weapons, and this book is dedicated to revealing what they are, but our first weapon should take a priority in our lives. The Word of God is vital to our survival. It was used by God to create the foundations of the entire universe and is also very intimate with the smallest detail of our lives. The Word of God shakes the very foundations of our problems. Romans 10:17 says that our faith is built upon by His Word. Our faith in the Word of God gives us strength and courage to go into battle.

Jeremiah 23:29 says that the Word is like a fire and a hammer. It burns out the impurities in our lives and breaks down the strongholds over us. If we properly use the Word of God to govern our lives we can eliminate many, if not all, of the heart aches that we suffer. We can use His Word to burn the chaff that draws us away from His presence and glory. We can also use His Word to break up the big burdens that really seem to weigh us down. Hebrews 4:12 says, "For the Word of God is living and powerful, and sharper than any two-edged sword, piercing even to the division of soul and spirit, and of joints and marrow, and is a discerner of the thoughts and intents of the heart." God's Word is the only weapon that can bring about change in our lives.

When Jesus was in the wilderness He used the Word of God to overcome Satan. Jesus was in a weakened state at the end of His forty-day fast. Satan recognized the situation and began to misuse the Word in an attempt to lure Jesus into a trap. When Satan began to use the Word, Jesus came back with the correct Word and understanding of that Word. Although He was weak from hunger, He was filled with the Word and the Spirit of God. He never forgot who He was and what His mission was. His ability to use the Word of God made Satan flee from His presence. We have the same authority to use God's Word against the enemy. When we come under attack, we are to rightly divide the Word of Truth and apply it to the situation. Rightly utilizing the Word will cause the enemy to flee.

One thing that we have to remember about using the Word of God as a weapon is this; other people are not the enemy. They are only used by the enemy to cause confusion and turmoil. God's Word should only be used to destroy the works of the enemy, not the people Satan uses to bring about disunity. The use of God's Word with people can be a little tricky. We will often use it as the hammer and beat them up. However, we also need to remember that the purpose of God's Word is to build His Kingdom rather than bring destruction upon His children. There may be times that we have to offend someone for the Word's sake, but we still have to come with the purpose of bringing loving correction. Trying to use one of the spiritual gifts without love just won't work. For God, love is the key to everything.

Second Timothy 3:16-17 says, "All Scripture is given by inspiration of God, and is profitable for doctrine, for reproof, for correction, for instruction in righteousness, [why] that the man of God may be complete, thoroughly equipped for every good work." If we use the Word of God incorrectly or with selfish motives, we will not be able to make the man of God in the perfect image of Jesus Christ. We will be destroying rather than building. The only way to build with the Word of God is if our mortar is the love of God.

Jesus said in John 6:63 the words that He speaks are spirit and they are life. We need to also speak life from the spirit and Word of God. He also said in John 12:49, "For I have not spoken on my own authority; but the Father who sent me gave me a command, what I should say and what I should speak." We also have the authority to speak God's Word, and there is a great responsibility to do so. We cannot treat His Word like a book of catch phrases. The Word is not to puff or lift us up; it is to lift up God. The Word must be given the honor it is due.

God spoke everything into existence with His Word. Everything exists because He is faithful to His Word. The Word of God contains nothing but truth and life. All life hangs in the balance of His Word. If the Word is that important to God, shouldn't we give much more consideration to it in our lives? Shouldn't we use it to guide us through the good and the bad times in our lives? Shouldn't we use it to encourage and exhort the body of Christ? Shouldn't we use it to draw the lost into a relationship with God? Shouldn't we use it to examine our own lives and make sure that we are in a right relationship with God? God's Word, mixed with the Holy Spirit, contains everything that we need to sustain our spiritual lives. God's Word is the source of life and contains all power to defeat the flesh and regenerate our spirits. His word destroys strongholds and will make us free. His Word will reconcile our relationship with Himself and others. And finally, His Word will bring joy to our hearts.

THE NAME OF JESUS

> In the beginning was the Word, and the Word
> was with God, and the Word was God. He was
> in the beginning with God. All things were
> made through Him; and without Him noth-
> ing was made that was made. In Him was Life;
> and the life was the light of men. And the light
> shines in darkness; and the darkness did not
> comprehend it.
>
> John 1:1-5

In the last chapter, I wrote that the Word of God is our most important weapon because on it rests all of our ability to overcome all darkness. In John chapter 1 we see that Jesus is the Word that was with God from the beginning. He is the co-creator of all things and in Him is light and life. His very name will either bring great joy or complete anger to those who hear it spoken. Our enemy shudders in fear at the mention of His name. Philippians 2:10-11 (KJV) says, "That at the name of Jesus every knee will bow and every tongue confess that Jesus Christ is Lord, to the glory of the Father." I could stop right now and be in awe of this reminder of the greatness of Jesus Christ. Regardless of how bad things can look to us, the fact remains that Jesus Christ is Lord.

When Jesus came near the demonic at the tombs, the demons inside of the man immediately recognized His authority. Jesus exercised the authority placed on Him from His Father. This is much the same way that the sickness reacted when Peter walked by. The anointing that God had placed on Peter was so strong that sickness had to flee from his presence. There wasn't anything about Peter that caused the sickness to flee. It was the fact that Peter walked in complete subjection to the Father and with the anointing that was placed on him, the sickness only recognized the person of Jesus walking by. Peter said in Acts 3:12 that it was not by his own power that the lame man was healed but the power and authority of Jesus, the one that they crucified. Like Peter, the apostles recognized that their works for God only worked through the name of Jesus. They understood that they had no power in themselves other than the name of Jesus.

Jesus said, "Verily, Verily, I say unto you, He that believes in me, the works that I do he will do; and greater works than these; because I go to my Father" (John 14:12). It is by His name and anointing that we operate in any of our spiritual gifts. Nothing is done from our own power or authority. It is true that many false teachers and prophets will perform signs and wonders in His name, but the Word clearly states that God must know the person using Jesus' name. Matthew 7:22-23 says, "Many will say to Me in that day, 'Lord, Lord, have we not prophesied in Your name, and done many wonders in Your name?' And then I will declare to them, 'I never knew you; depart from me, you workers of lawlessness.'" So what is the difference between a true believer in Christ and a false prophet or teacher? If both will do signs and wonders, what is the separating factor between them. The difference is being "known" by the Father. True believers have a real saving knowledge of Jesus while false prophets and teachers do not. True believers are bound with the desire to bring glory to God and not upon themselves. While I am not a judge concerning the hearts of men, I believe that false prophets and teachers place their motivation on self promotion and fulfillment. Because of this, God will say, "I never knew you." We must have the motivation of advancing the kingdom of God and bringing Him glory when we use the name of Jesus.

I can remember a testimony of a friend who once had a bad dream. In the dream, which seemed very real to him, he was under severe demonic attack. He could not move a muscle because he was bound from head to toe. The only thing that he could do was whisper the name of Jesus. After his first whisper, the demons that had him bound seemed to tremble a little, so he whispered "Jesus" again. The demons trembled even more. The more that he said the name of Jesus, it came out stronger and the demons began to shake violently in fear until they could not take it anymore. The demons had to flee at the name of Jesus. When he awakened from his dream, his faith in the name of Jesus had grown tremendously. As believers, we have the same authority to use the name of Jesus. When using His name with the authority granted to us, demons will flee.

We, God's church, have been given a great responsibility to do the work of our Father on this earth, but even a greater responsibility to use the name of Jesus as the very authority for what we do for Him. The entire Word of God is centered on the name of Jesus. Everything we do must also be centered on the name of Jesus. If we have a ministry, Jesus must be the focus of all of our glory. He must be the center of our authority.

Acts 17:28 says, "For in Him we live and move and have our being, as also some of your own poets have said, 'For we are His offspring.'" Jesus is the author and the finisher of our faith. His death on the cross and His resurrection to the right hand of the Father put all things back into the proper balance in our relationship with Him. He did it all. It is by Him that we can minister and by Him that we are called. The very God that breathed life into Adam and Eve has breathed His spirit into us so we could and still do those greater works that Jesus spoke about in John 14:12. These greater works must be done only in the name of Jesus.

OBEDIENCE

After reading about the sin of Adam and Eve, I understood something about the Lord that I hadn't realized before. God really enjoyed His fellowship with Adam and Eve. It seems like God frequently walked in the garden to have fellowship with them. This is noted in Genesis 3:7 when they saw that they were naked and needed to cover themselves. Did they know it was time for God to take His walk through the garden? We can't say for sure, but it does seem so. Their fall to temptation and attempt to hide it from God reveals to us that we cannot pay our sin debt. God had to make a sacrifice to cover their sin. This sacrifice did not redeem Adam and Eve at all. They were covered without redemption, and they were still banished from the garden.

In 1 Samuel 15:22-23, God had commanded King Saul to destroy Amalek. Saul was instructed to slay all of the men, women, infants and children, the sheep, oxen, fattened calves, the lambs, and all that was good. Nothing was to be kept alive. When King Saul's army was finished, they had spared King Agag, the best of the sheep, fatlings, oxen, the lambs, and all that was good. Everything that was despised and worthless was destroyed. The Lord immediately sent word to Samuel that He was displeased with Saul. Saul told Samuel that he spared the best of the animals to offer a sacrifice before the Lord. In verse 22, Samuel told Saul, "Does the Lord as great a delight in burnt offerings and sacrifices, as in obeying the voice of the Lord? Behold, to obey is better than sacrifice, and to hearken than the fat of rams." Verse 23: "For rebellion is as the sin of witchcraft, and stubbornness is as iniquity and idolatry. Because you have rejected the Word of the Lord, He has also rejected you from being king." God would rather have a people with obedient hearts than have the need for continual sacrifices.

Another example is found in 2 Samuel 12 when Nathan rebuked King David for his actions with Bathsheba and Uriah. In verse 13 we find an interesting occurrence; after Nathan rebuked him, Kind David just repented. He said, "I have sinned against the Lord." There was no sacrifice, no altar, and no high priest, just a man with a broken heart laid out before the Lord. Nathan told David that the Lord had put his sin away. There were consequences to come because, as Nathan said, he gave occasion for the enemies to blaspheme the Lord and his child would also die. The seeds were planted for a bad crop to grow; however, the sin was wiped clean.

We can read story after story throughout the Word of God and see examples where people disobeyed the Lord to fulfill the lust of the flesh. With that said, we see the same things in the lives of our friends as if they were performing Bible reenactments. It is so easy to be the one looking into a situation and see the impending destruction. Yet, when it comes to our own lives, it is much harder to see the danger signs of rebellion and sin pulling us away from serving God with our highest potential. When we finally realize that we are 180 degrees in the opposite direction, we tend to act like Adam and Eve and sew fig leaves together to cover our sin. Or we will blame someone else for the sin in our lives.

As believers in Christ, we know that this is not what God wants for us. We understand that Jesus came to die to bring the redemption to us that the sacrifice in the garden could not bring. We understand that we live under the shadow of God's grace and mercy rather than His more immediate rule and judgment. We understand all of this but still run away from His grace most of the time. Our victory comes when we can tell the tempter that we are bought with a price and do not want any part of his trash. However, we can also proclaim victory when we run under that shadow of His wings with repentance. The Lord will put our sin away just as He did with David. It is no different from when we first became born again. The slate is wiped clean.

Since we, man, had fallen into a sinful nature, we could not act in true obedience to the Lord. It is true that there are a lot of good things that we do in our lives, but none of them can measure up to the true goodness of God. We cannot, of our own accord, act in enough obedience toward God without having a saving knowledge of Jesus' own sacrifice for us. Our flesh cannot obey, without His spirit, and Jesus could not disobey. His perfect obedience was two things for us: 1) It was our only chance to have a sacrifice good enough to bring our redemption to God. Hebrews 9:12-14 says, "Not by the blood of goats and calves, but with His own blood He entered the Most Holy Place once and for all, having obtained eternal redemption. For if the blood of bulls and goats and the ashes of a heifer, sprinkled the unclean, sanctifies for the purifying of the flesh, how much more shall the blood of Christ, who through the eternal Spirit offered Himself without spot to God, cleanse your conscience from dead works to serve the living God?" 2) His obedience was our perfect example to follow as we go through this life on earth. Romans 5:19 says, "For as by one man's disobedience many were made sinners, so also by one Man's obedience many will be made righteous."

It is difficult for the public at large to understand that "I am a good person" can't measure up to God's goodness or Jesus' perfect obedience. God cannot accept anything other than perfect obedience. Even Christians can't fulfill that order, but we can enter in under the shadow of Jesus and His obedience.

Yes, obedience is better than sacrifice, but it is by His obedience in the sacrifice that we can truly please God.

FAITH

Webster's dictionary states that faith is: A belief and trust in and loyalty to God, belief in the traditional doctrines of a religion, firm belief in something for which there is no proof, complete trust.

By definition, we should have complete trust and loyalty to God even though, by the world's standards, we have no proof of His existence. As believers, we can see plenty of proof in all that God has created. Everything that He created has a unity and equilibrium that science can barely grasp and understand. It just requires us to look through a biblical periscope to see His handy work. A periscope is used to provide a different vantage point from current circumstances. Just like a submarine needs a periscope to look beyond its present surroundings, believers need to use the Word of God as a periscope to look beyond their surroundings and/or circumstances.

The definition says that faith is a belief in the traditional doctrine of a religion. Unfortunately, we have to wrestle with manmade doctrines. John 1:1 says, "In the beginning was the Word and the Word was with God, and the Word was God." Just as Genesis is the foundation for how God created everything, John 1:1

sets the precedent that God's Word is the beginning of all things. As believers, we understand that this verse is also talking about Jesus. We can believe this because Genesis 1:26 say's, "Let us make man in our image ... " and implies that the Trinity was working together during the time of creation. Romans 10:17 says, "So then, faith comes by hearing, and hearing by the Word of God." Our level of faith is a direct reflection of how much of God's Word we allow to penetrate our spirit. It is impossible to grow in faith if we don't grow in the Word. Hebrew 11:6 says, "But without faith it is impossible to please Him, for he who comes to God must believe that He is, and that He is a rewarder of those who diligently seek Him." We must get into His Word because when times are difficult, we can believe that He is. If we seek Him diligently, we will grow and please Him as well. As we grow in His Word we will fulfill Hebrews 11:1, which says, "Now faith is the substance of things hoped for, the evidence of things not seen." When we can believe in Him and His word without blinking an eye, we will be able to stand against the enemy.

We don't usually have a hard time expressing our faith when things are going well, but what do we do when the world starts to raise the heat a little? I'm not even talking the kind of heat placed on Shadrach, Meshach, and Abednego. Most of us probably won't go through a trial of that magnitude; however, I won't try to minimize any trial of the saints of God. Their faith, along with many others throughout God's Word, was a special kind of faith. It's a place that most of us can only dream of. What do I mean? I have heard it said, by me as well, "I wish that I had that kind of faith," or "If I go through anything like that, I hope I can pass the test." I have even said, "I hope that I would never go through something like that." Romans 12:3 says that God has given every man a measure of faith. You could say that this is a faith starter kit. He gives enough of a measure of faith to work with so we can make it grow. It is in much the same way that the master distributed the talents to his servants. He gave them talents to work and produce more talents. God desires to see the faith that He gave to us grow. The only way we can have the kind of faith that Shadrach, Meshach, and Abednego had is to exercise that faith into a strong, healthy muscle. The more we exercise that muscle, the stronger that it will get.

David did not slay Goliath with a smooth stone. Sure, he took five smooth stones from a brook, loaded his sling and hurled that stone into Goliaths forehead, but it was His faith that leveled the giant. David was fully armed with a faith in God that proved too great for Goliath. David could have had a hundred stones, but if he was not built up in faith, if God had not allowed him to be tested before the bigger battle, he could not have stood against Goliath. You see—our battle yesterday will help us get prepared for the battle tomorrow.

Let me give you an example. When my brother and I were in high school we ran cross-country and track. We were fairly evenly matched in the sprint runs, but he could leave me behind on the distance runs. Why? He spent a lot of time preparing for the competitions.

When he was a junior, he began training for a marathon. He had to spend a lot of time running to get prepared. The funny thing is this—he could never run the full 26.21 miles while he was training. I believe that his longest distance was just over eighteen miles.

On the day of the race, he seemed confident in his training to get to the end. I think there was one thing that actually helped him get through the competition. As he was getting prepared, he spent most of his time running alone, and this time he had hundreds of people going toward the prize with him. My dad and I were keeping track of him and during the last ten miles or so, my brother passed 116 people. We were amazed. We would have been just as proud if he did not pass them or if he had even fallen back. He never said, "I don't think that I can do this because I couldn't do it during my training." He may not have run twenty-six miles before, but he did it that day. Dad and I were so proud of him.

Well, what does this have to do with faith? If you will remember, God is the Alpha and the Omega, the beginning and the end. He knows what lies ahead for us and He desires for us to be prepared. During these times of preparation, the enemy is trying to derail our faith in God while God is working at molding us into His image. When David fought Goliath he had never fought a giant before; however, God allowed him to get prepared with the use of a lion and a bear. It was in those times that God had built his faith up for the next battle. He never said, "I have never fought a giant before, I don't think that I can do this." He made a proclamation that he killed that lion and the bear and the giant would fall at his hand as well. We don't know what our next battle will be, but we must believe that God will anoint us to do things that we have never done before. When we go into battle we attain victory in the strength of the Lord and not our own strength.

Another thing about our faith is that it cannot be built up by the things of this world. As David was getting prepared to fight Goliath, King Saul offered him his armor and sword. It wasn't just the fact that Saul's armor did not fit David but the armor was specifically built for Saul. What David knew was this: God was his armor, God was his strong tower, and God was his strength and refuge. He knew that God was his glory and the lifter of his head. God was the one that would go before him into battle.

The desire of God is for us to have the kind of faith in Him that we desire more of Him in our lives. It is God's desire to have that kind of relationship with us. He wants nothing more than to have our faith sold out for His glory. A faith that is committed to God not only pleases Him but causes us to remain encouraged and provide encouragement to others. Our faith is the key to the gifts that God has provided to us. It will unlock them for use that will build up the kingdom of God.

LOVE

Love in our own understanding can take on many forms and ideals but is only defined by three words. When the words eros love, philia love and agape love are read, it is hard to imagine that any form of love can be used as a weapon of warfare. With that said, it is sometimes because of love that people will engage in war. In America it is hard to define what love truly is because we have such a distorted view of love. We say that we love everything. We love our pets, we love different foods, we love the cars we drive, etc. In reality, we don't really love any of those things, but we do like them at a very high level. It is hard for us to visualize what true love looks like, but by the end of this chapter, I pray that we have a better understanding. And with that understanding we will see how love can be used as a weapon of warfare.

Most of us can identify with eros and philia because they define how we deal with others through relationships. Eros defines our relationships with others on a more intimate level. When we say, "I'm in love," it usually comes from the eros form of love. This form of love has been abused and turned inside out, and we mistakenly use it to define almost all forms of love. People who mistakenly think they are in love will be destroyed by wrong relationships. There are so many people who remain in wrong relationships because they are told that they are loved. This errant form of eros is not love at all. This would be described as bondage. Real love is not a form of bondage. Eros is, in part, based on our emotions.

Philia is described as friendship love, or brotherly love. People who enjoy the intimate company of their friends are exercising philia. One problem that I see in philia is the friendships that are tagged with guilt. One friend will say to the other friend, "If you like me, you will do this." Just like eros, this kind of action in a friendship is a form of bondage. True friendships are adorned with the freedom of being who we are, without the need to change for someone else. We made friends with someone because we saw an attribute that we thought was worth our time and effort to spend time with. It is also the philia that will allow us to stand up for one of our friends if they are under attack. We will offer protection to a friend who we think needs help.

The one problem with eros and philia is the fact that they are based on our emotions. Our emotions can be like a roller coaster ride when the circumstances of our lives vary from day to day. Our emotions will dictate who we like or how we treat others, based on how we are feeling that particular day. If the one we love has done something to make us mad, our eros is strained and possibly broken. If a friend or group of friends failed to invite us to a gathering, our philia is hurt, and we wonder if the friendships are worth the hassle.

These two types of love also struggle with the temptation of the new relationship. What I mean is this: someone who looks better, or the group of friends who seem to be cooler than our current friends can make us trade our eros/philia from one person, or group, for another. We have detached our feelings fairly easily in these circumstances. Eros and philia do distort the true purpose and meaning of how God intended real love to be.

Agape is God's love. It is a love not devoid of emotion, but it is not based on emotion. Agape does not look at the circumstances to see if someone else deserves our love. Agape does not promote itself over others. Agape is not jealous of others. Agape encourages others to be successful even if it means that we don't get a promotion. Agape offers forgiveness every time it is needed. Agape is the greatest gift that God has given us through His Holy Spirit because it is with this love that all of the other gifts operate. It is the key ingredient toward spiritual success. When we operate in agape, others will see Christ in us. Agape is a weapon of our warfare because it causes us to always stand up for what is right. It causes us to fight for the needs of others without any benefit of reward. It was by agape that Jesus displayed the full measure of the glory of God, even on the cross.

As we have been discussing, 2 Corinthians 10:4 says that our weapons are not carnal. In other words, they are not formed by the hands of man. God is the originator of love, but we have been used by the enemy of our souls to distort His purpose for love. It is in much the same way that our original purpose has been distorted. As we will learn, the original purpose of love and man can only be corrected through the sacrifice of Jesus Christ.

In Luke 22, Jesus went to the garden of Gethsemane to pray. As with all of His time in prayer, this time in the garden was used as a time of preparation. Jesus spent a lot of time in prayer, and I believe that He used that time to hear His Father's voice and prepare for working in the anointing of the Holy Spirit. Jesus was in much need of this preparation because He was getting ready to face His biggest challenge. The unleashing of the enemy was going to be horrendous and He needed the strength and encouragement of His Father.

As Jesus was praying, the agony of the moment was very great. We all know that Jesus was God incarnate, but the weight of the sin that was going to bear down on Him was a heavy load. He knew His purpose and the joy that was set before Him, but that did not prevent the amount of turmoil with which He had to wrestle. Jesus did not give in to the torment but submitted His agony to the perfect love of the Father. He placed His own body on the cross of pain, shame, and death for the sin of all mankind. He put on full display the pure, non-carnal nature of God's love for each one of us. To further illustrate my point, a servant of Jesus cut off the ear of a soldier who came to arrest Jesus. Jesus could have taken a sword as well but chose to do the unthinkable instead. Instead of fighting with the carnal nature, He chose to submit Himself to the love of God and healed the soldier. When Jesus went to the cross, He put His flesh in subjection to the non-carnal love of His Father.

In Luke 18:31-34 Jesus said:

> Behold, we go up to Jerusalem, and all things that are written by the prophets concerning the Son of man shall be accomplished. For He shall be delivered unto the Gentiles, and shall be mocked, and spitefully entreated, and spit upon: And they shall scourge Him, and put Him to death: and on the third day He shall rise again.

This almost seems like a passing thought that the disciples did not understand. Jesus did not make a long discourse about the events that were about to happen. He did not tell His disciples to take up the sword and fight for His honor. He made that statement and moved on with His Father's work. When Jesus stood before His accusers, He never spoke words of condemnation. When He was being beaten, He never raised a hand in His defense or tried to fight back. When He was on the cross He could have allowed His flesh to cry out for the heavenly host of angels to destroy those that brought on this misery. Jesus did not do anything to defend His own honor or character because He knew that it was for the glory of His Father and the joy that was set before Him. That joy was you and I, having the reconnected purpose with the Father and Creator of all. God's love so permeated Jesus that it enabled Him to desire God to forgive them because they did not know what they were doing. The people did not fully understand the purpose of Jesus and the intended sacrifice that He needed to make. Through the agony of the cross and the burden of sin, He cried out for forgiveness rather than retaliation.

I am also reminded of the woman caught in the act of adultery. We don't really know her story except for what is written in God's Word. We don't know if she was a prostitute or a woman caught up in a bad relationship. Whatever the case may be her accusers used her to seek an opportunity to set a trap for Jesus. Regardless of her circumstances, she had a distorted view of love. It cannot go without saying that the man she was with had the same distorted view of love as well. In her weakness and vulnerability she was used as bait and was humiliated before her accusers and Jesus. That is exactly what Satan does as well. He will promise us the world to get what he wants, but when he is finished with us, he will play the accuser of the brethren. He does not have an ounce of love or mercy in his entire being. The woman caught in adultery did not know what true love looked like. She confused sex and passion for love. It was not until she was brought before Jesus that she saw how love was supposed to work in her life. She learned that through proper love comes proper purpose. Her enemy was sent packing by the love of Jesus. The love of Christ enables God's purpose to rise within us and draw us toward the perfect image of His Son.

In Matthew 26:69-75 Peter was confronted as being a follower of Jesus. Three times accused and three times denied. After the rooster crowed, Peter knew what he had done. I am sure that he felt hopeless and in despair.

It wasn't too long before this that Jesus told His disciples, "If any man desires to come after me, let him deny himself, and take up his cross, and follow me" (Matthew 16:24). Peter was probably thinking, "He told me to deny myself and yet I denied Him." How many times have we denied Jesus rather than ourselves? The great thing about this set of passages is the fact that Jesus refused to let Peter stay lost and broken. After the resurrection, Jesus poured His love over Peter. Read John 21:15-19.

God's ability to share His perfect love has been given to us by His Holy Spirit. His gifts and calling are without repentance (Romans 11:29), but His gifts and calling only work by love. His love for others through us is how they will see the kingdom of God. It is how we can be used to set others free from their bondage, as well as allowing the Holy Spirit to keep us from getting into bondage. When Paul and Silas were beaten and jailed, they were able to display God's love toward the jailer in such a miraculous way it allowed them to bring him and his family to the saving knowledge of Jesus Christ. Their faith and love of the Father shook the foundations of the enemies grip on them. The anointing was so strong that the other prisoners could not leave the presence of God. We too can affect that kind of change in the lives of others. God's Word is not just a book full of stories about how He used other people a long time ago. His Word is full of examples of how we can be used by the Lord to radically change our churches, places of employment, and the regions in which we live.

Brothers and sisters, each of us has a calling from the Lord. However, the enemy does everything he can to make us minimize what we can do for the kingdom of God. He does this by getting us to doubt that God can use us. He gets us to believe that we have made too many mistakes to be used. He gets us to believe that our problems are too big for God to work through. Ultimately, he gets us to forget how much God really loves us.

Saints of God, everything that God has done and will do is centered on the fact that He loves us without measure. His love runs so deep that the "River of Living Water" has love as its source. Although this phrase is first mentioned in John chapter 4, we have to remember that Jesus transcends time (John 1:1). He never said anything that was not already present in heaven. My friends, if we can begin to allow love to be the source of all of our labors, our attitude, and our whole being, we will see great victory in our lives. We will begin to see lives changed for the glory of God and the advancement of His kingdom. When His love permeates who we are, we will begin to reflect the image of Jesus Christ that God has desired from the beginning. And the world will no longer be confused by the message that we send. Our message will be Jesus Christ alone, which is the only message of hope for being an over comer in this world. So let the light of His love be the light that guides you through to victory.

FORGIVENESS

There is one thing that destroys friendships, marriages, families, and churches more than any other thing: unforgiveness. Unforgiveness is a crippling act of self that drives a wedge in every relationship that we have. It also puts a heavy burden on us as we attempt to carry the load of sin. In part, it is why people who make the decision to give their hearts to Jesus feel such a release of the heaviness that has been covering them. God's grace (forgiveness), our unmerited favor, climaxed with the death, burial, and resurrection of Jesus. I wrote about how obedience causes God to move on our behalf. Forgiveness is the one thing we do that mirrors who God is, more so than anything else that we can do. It encompasses the act of love. It requires faith to forgive. It is an act of worship to God. It requires humility to perform.

As you can see, it takes a lot for us to forgive. So many things come into play when we enact forgiveness for someone. Yet, if we do not forgive, God will not forgive us. This is so powerfully written in Matthew 18:21-35. Jesus spoke about an unjust servant who would not forgive his debtor after he had been forgiven of a much greater debt. In Matthew 18:35, Jesus said,

"So My heavenly Father also will do to you if each of you, from his heart, does not forgive his brother his trespasses." That is a strong condemnation. Now, you may be thinking of Romans 8:1 when it says, "There is therefore now no condemnation to those who are in Christ Jesus." I would have to say that you are correct if I let you stop there, but the verse goes on to say this, "who do not walk according to the flesh, but according to the Spirit." When we harbor unforgiveness toward someone, we are walking according to the flesh. So that leads to condemnation from God and does not enable us to hold onto Romans 8:1.

There is a real danger when we are unwilling to forgive another person's mistakes. First of all, it automatically separates us from God. In other words, it places us in the position of being apart from God. He will never leave us or forsake us, but we can leave Him. If someone, whether on purpose or on accident, causes you harm, they have placed a heavy burden on themselves and you. At this point, there are choices that have to be made. If the person realizes their mistake and asks for your forgiveness, they have asked for a release from their weight. If you decide not to forgive them, you have actually held on to your weight while taking on theirs also. When a person has asked for forgiveness, they have accepted their responsibility for the mess they have made. Your choice is deciding if you both get to lay down your weights. When both parties get to lay their weights down, everyone walks away with more power. Unforgiveness also breeds other spiritual problems. Not only do you have the weight of two people's sins, but you are entangled by the works of the flesh.

Unforgiveness causes us to live in the flesh. Galatians 5:19-21 says:

> Now the works of the flesh are evident, which are: adultery, fornication, uncleanness, lewdness, idolatry, sorcery, hatred, contentions, jealousies, outbursts of wrath, selfish ambitions, dissensions, heresies, envy, murders, drunkenness, revelries, and the like; of which I tell you beforehand, just as I also told you in time past, that those who practice such things will not inherit the kingdom of God.

When we are bound by the sin of unforgiveness, we are susceptible to letting other spiritual problems jump on us.

Is the pride of being right in an argument worth being separated from God? Are your hurt feelings keeping you from a relationship with God or someone that should be a close friend? Are you letting bitterness separate you from a church member or a family member? Is it time to let go of something that is holding you back from fully serving the Lord? I would think that now is the time.

I should mention here that there is a flip side to not forgiving someone when they ask. There are those times when you will have it on your heart to forgive a wrong before someone asks, or even when someone refuses to ask for forgiveness. If you can wipe their slate clean and release them from their burden, God gets immediate glory, and you have deepened your relationship with

God. Stephen did this in Acts 7:60. He said, "Lord, do not charge them with this sin." He was releasing them from their sin without their asking. I am certain that they felt justified by their actions, but I believe that Stephen's release bought them time for God to deal with them individually. I can remember times when God has dealt with me to forgive in this manner. When I forgave the person, I felt so liberated from the burden of their sin. It also allowed me to maintain a relationship with the person that brought the offense. I won't say that it will always be easy, but if you allow God the opportunity, He will renew your spirit.

It is said that God is love, but that love is demonstrated best through forgiveness. We demonstrate God's love through forgiveness. God heals relationships through forgiveness. How many friendships, marriages, families, and churches would have remained intact if forgiveness was applied? Proverbs 16:18 says, "Pride goes before destruction, and a haughty spirit before a fall."

It is better to lose a battle and maintain a relationship than to win at all costs and lose everything. That does not mean that we should waver with the Word of God. We should never compromise with the Word; however, we need to be mindful of those things that are eternal and those things that are not. We are ambassadors for Christ. Can we say that we love Him and withhold forgiveness? Faith without works is dead, and forgiveness is a work of our faith in God. It is a wonderful weapon that destroys the work of the enemy.

Forgiveness, though, is best illustrated by Jesus Himself. He willingly bore the punishment for our sins so we could be put back into a right relationship with God the Father. God has such a deep, affectionate love for us that He could not bear being separated from His most precious creation. Our sins had to be paid for, and we could not pay the debt. We were destined for eternal separation from God if He did not intervene. His love for us was greater than the power of sin and separation. His grace was epitomized at the cross of Christ. His glory was powerfully made manifest at the resurrection of Jesus. It was the power of God, through the Holy Spirit that raised Jesus from the dead. The resurrection powerfully revealed the omnipotence of God and control over death and hell. It is why we believe that God reigns supreme in the first place. The act of forgiveness originates from heaven. If anyone, saved or lost, forgives, they are imitating God whether they know it or not.

Jesus told Peter in Matthew 18:22 that we ought to forgive up to seventy times seven. How many times has God had to forgive us of our sins? To be more specific, how many times has He forgiven the same sin? If it is our desire to become like Christ, we must forgive. We are so ready to receive the grace and forgiveness of God but what about extending His grace and forgiveness toward others? That is sometimes very difficult to do, but who are we to withhold forgiveness when God sent His only Son, Jesus, to pay our sin debt? Are we better than God to think that we don't have to forgive? Jesus died for the sins of everyone so we must be willing to forgive everyone. If you want to release the power of God in your life, then you must forgive.

PRAYER

Of all the weapons that we have at our disposal, prayer would have to be the most difficult for us to use and comprehend. I'm reminded of a scene from the movie version of The Little Rascals. The scene begins when the "He-Man Woman Haters" clubhouse catches on fire. Pee Wee and Buckwheat run to the nearest phone to get help. They patiently wait their turn and when it finally comes, Buckwheat says, "Quick, what's the number for 911?" As the camera pulls back, the two walk away from the pay phone and we see that the fire department was right across the street. Does this sound a lot like your prayer life? It greatly resembles mine too much of the time. A desperate need jumps out at us and we can't seem to remember God's number; all the while He is right there beside us.

When Jesus and His disciples went into the garden of Gethsemane to pray, Jesus came back to His disciples and found them asleep. At this point, He said something that I think most people miss from the context of the scripture. He said in Mark 14:38, "Watch and pray, lest you enter into temptation. The spirit indeed is willing, but the flesh is weak." There are several things about prayer that I think Jesus is trying to teach His disciples. 1) We need to always watch for the move or attacks of the enemy. We need to be very diligent about our soul as if we are a walled city with watchmen in each tower, looking out for enemy movement. We also need to be always looking out for God and the move of His hand. Although we won't necessarily see Him working on our behalf, we need to trust that He is. 2) Combined with watching, we need to pray. Why do these go hand in hand? When we are watching or on the lookout, we need to pray for strength when the enemy does come in with a full assault. The assault can come in the open or in stealth mode. We also need to pray for invitation to join in God's presence and to work around us. The more often we are joined into what God is doing, we will be centered into His will and forsake our own fleshly desires. It does not mean that attacks won't come, but we will be focused on God more than the attempt being made to distract us from God.

Jesus also said that watching and praying will prepare us for the coming temptations. If we are in a state of prayer and communion with God, we will find that His presence is more enjoyable than anything offered by the enemy. But, Jesus also shared an insight that we are always in a spiritual fight. We have an everyday decision between allowing our spirit man to control what we do and giving in to the flesh. God understands that our spirit is willing, but it is not enough to be always willing and never doing. The weapon of obedience is very critical with prayer, in the context of Jesus speaking in the garden.

We need to understand that willingness without obedience is like having faith without works. James 2:20, 26 says that faith without works is dead. So, too, is willingness without obedience. Obedience is the action of willingness.

The disciples had a hard time maintaining their commitment to Jesus in prayer. Although Jesus was probably frustrated with His disciples at the time, He really wanted them, and us, to understand that being prepared for the entanglements of life comes by prayer. We see this truth played out throughout the Bible. Daniel was in a constant state of prayer. When he was told to only pray to the king, he knew that God was the only source of help that he had. Jesus went off to be alone to pray a lot. His prayer time was very critical for His ministry. Paul and Silas prayed and sang praises in jail. Those prayers allowed them to focus on God rather than their situation. As a result, the jailer and his family were saved and brought into the kingdom of God. In Acts chapter 12 we see that Peter was freed from prison because those in the church "prayed without ceasing." God has greatly illustrated that He desires to have an intimate relationship with us. Prayer is probably the easiest way for us to return to intimacy with God.

Let's get back to my first example from The Little Rascals. When we have walked away or not maintained our relationship with God, we tend to throw 911 prayers at Him. These prayers do not develop a relationship with God. They can develop into an intimate relationship as the needs and prayers get more consistent and personal. The hurdle of guilt seems too high for us becoming intimate in our prayer life. We feel inadequate because we never feel like we are praying enough. I can honestly say that no one prays enough. Sometimes it is because we don't think that we can hear God's voice. Trust me, you can. We tend to listen to the wrong voice though. The voice that says, "You're not good enough. You don't pray enough. You're a hypocrite." That is the voice of the enemy. The Word of God says that we are loved, accepted, a royal priesthood, the body of Christ, etc. That is the voice of God. Yes, God does desire a relationship with each one of us, but not at the expense of destroying your esteem. God sent Jesus to die on the cross so we could be in right relationship with Him. He would not take on the punishment for sin and then ridicule and belittle you for having weaknesses. We cannot measure up to God's standards on our own. God doesn't measure us by others either. We are measured by the standard of the cross. The great thing about that is this: when we stand behind the cross our faults and shortcomings are hidden by the blood of the lamb that was slain.

People also have problems praying because they think that they have nothing to pray about. Here is a list of things to get you started: Our president, your church & pastor(s), city, state, and country, other elected officials, your family, your child's school, your neighbors, and co-workers. These are just a few things to pray for. I encourage you to stand before God and develop your relationship with Him in prayer. Remember; listen for the voice of the Holy Spirit, and He will be encouraging you all the way.

FASTING

Second Corinthians 10:4 states, "For the weapons of our warfare are not carnal, but mighty through God to the pulling down of strong holds." Fasting, however, incorporates our flesh into a weapon of war. As with the other weapons, fasting cannot be formed by the hands of man. As a matter of fact, it is quite the opposite. Our flesh must be sustained with food that has been forged by the work of a man. With fasting, we are denying our flesh its normal routine of food for the sake of the kingdom of God. We are actually giving ourselves completely over to God for a period of time so that He may use us for His purpose in His kingdom. You may be asking how this could be used as a weapon. Satan tempts us through the five senses of sight, smell, taste, touch, and hearing. We are commanded many times to walk after the spiritual things and forsake the flesh. God does know that we have need of food, but there are times when He calls us to even deny ourselves of food. Although there are many things that can be denied during a fast, food is the most common.

There are many examples covering several types of fasts throughout the Bible. There were fasts of mourning, sorrow, repentance, and anxiety, to name a few.

David fasted when his son was ill. Esther fasted and called for all Jews to fast when she prepared to expose the sin of Haman. Jesus fasted while in the desert to prepare Himself for the work of God. Satan brought his temptations to Jesus while he was fasting and at a very physically weak state. Jesus overcame the temptations by the Word of God and complete submission to His Father.

In Matthew 17:14-21, Jesus casts a devil out of the boy that was often thrown into the fire, and then water. The boy's father took him to the disciples of Jesus, but they could not cast the devil out. Jesus told His disciples several things that they lacked, starting with a lack of faith. In verse 21, Jesus went into a deeper explanation of spiritual warfare. He said, "However, this kind does not go out except by prayer and fasting." Jesus was not saying that prayer was not an effective weapon. It just needed more power behind it.

Here is an example from physical warfare. For a long time, our military developed rocket propelled bombs that could cause a lot of damage. These bombs caused the enemy to take notice, but not until World War II did a bomb with an atomic warhead cause a nation to surrender as quickly as Japan did. The atomic power added to a normal bomb multiplied its intensity. This is what fasting does to prayer. Prayer is a great weapon that moves mountains in the spiritual world with only a little bit of faith. When we fast, we are showing the entire spirit world that we have great faith and we mean business.

When we deny our flesh, we are committing our complete trust to God. It is one of the highest forms of worship. As I stated at the beginning, we are denying our flesh for the purpose of the kingdom of God.

Jesus made some clear statements concerning the fast. In Matthew 6:16-18, He said that the hypocrites show a sad countenance so they could reap sympathy as they appeared to be fasting. We are to anoint our heads and wash our face and let no one know that we are fasting. We should not be looking for reward or sympathy for the sake of our fasting. Our reward comes only from heaven. He made another statement concerning public fasting when He spoke about the publican and the Pharisee. The Pharisee made it a point to tell God and the publican how good he was by his loud boasting of fasting twice a week. The publican would not even raise his eyes toward heaven, with nothing to offer but a repentant heart. Jesus said that the publican was justified more than the Pharisee.

Matthew 25:31-40 is not usually attributed to fasting, but please allow me an opportunity to explain. In this scripture, Jesus says, starting in verse 35, "for I was hungry and you gave me food; I was thirsty and you gave me drink; I was a stranger and you took me in; I was naked and you clothed me; I was sick and you visited me; I was in prison and you came to me." You might be asking yourself how this lines up with fasting. In Isaiah 58:1-9, Isaiah wrote about the type of fast that pleases God. Beginning in verse 6, God told Isaiah:

> Is this not the fast that I have chosen: To loose the bonds of wickedness, to undo the heavy burdens, to let the oppressed go free, and to break every yoke? Is it not to share your bread with the hungry, and to bring to your house the poor who are cast out; when you see the naked, that you cover him, and not hide yourself in your own flesh?

Pay attention to what He says next. In verse 8, He went on to say:

> Then your light shall break forth like the morning. Your healing shall spring forth speedily. And your righteousness shall go before you: The glory of the Lord shall be your rear guard. Then you shall cry, and the Lord will answer; you shall cry, and He will say, "Here I am."

As I see it now, fasting works by our physical surrender to God, and our service toward others. Our love for God will be made manifest toward Him and those around us with a fast directed by Him. God will be glorified while others are being blessed.

When we fast, we are not to follow a particular formula. We are to follow the Word of God. God may call you to fast for a period of time, but you should remember a few things. 1) Keep your fast between you and God. Your call to a fast is no one else's business. 2) When you fast, be prepared for attacks of temptations. You will be in a physically weakened state and the enemy knows it. Your victory will come with the Word of God. 3) When you fast, offer yourself for the work of ministry. Minister to others as the Lord leads you. 4) Fasting is not a ritual. A fast is a call to worship. God may have you fast on certain days, but make sure that you are called to do so. This warning basically fits with any call of God. Make sure that it is God calling you. Don't set yourself up to following "good works." Jesus warned in Matthew 7:21-23:

> Not everyone that says to me, Lord, Lord, shall enter into the kingdom of heaven; but he that does the will of my Father in heaven. Many will say to me in that day, 'Lord, Lord, have we not prophesied in Your name, cast out demons in Your name and done many wonders in Your name?' And then will I declare to them, I never knew you: depart from me, you who practice lawlessness.

We show our faith by our works toward God and furthering His kingdom. As a weapon, fasting is like adding a nuclear warhead to our faith, our worship, our prayers, and our obedience. It is a testimony to God that we love Him and trust Him with everything that He has given us, including our bodies.

PRAISE

We are to the point that the weapons of our warfare are beginning to intermingle. To clarify, all of our weapons can and should be used together, but it seems that certain weapons are like bread and butter. They just go together. You should be able to read this book and think of a time when you used two or three weapons to overcome something. As you read each chapter, don't lock yourself into a particular weapon thinking that it will solve all of your problems, remind yourself of them all and use each of them as needed.

God is very adamant that His saints offer Him praise. He does not want praise because it boosts His ego. That is what we do when we seek the praise of others. God knows exactly who He is. He desires praise because He loves us. He desires an intimate relationship with his creation. The thing about praise is being able to offer it any time. I have been to several churches that had a time set aside for "Praise Reports." Most of these praise reports were offered to God for meeting a need such as money, a job, healing, etc. It is so awesome to hear about God's provision because they encourage the faith of others. The praise reports that get little mention are these: "I praise God for who He is" and "I praise God for His infinite mercy."

Any kind of praise offering is good, but what touches the heart of God are the praises declaring His majesty. When we can praise Him because of His majesty instead of His provision we have trusted His heart rather than what is in His hand. The reason for this is because praising Him for His provision can go lacking when we can't see Him providing what we think we need. If we can't see God in our situation, we have difficulty offering praises. Offering praises for what God provides could be called "Provisional Praise."

David offers many insights to how we should praise God through his psalms. I obviously don't have enough room in this chapter to give you all of his examples, but I will share a few.

Psalm 7:17—"I will praise the Lord according to His righteousness: and will sing praise to the name of the Lord Most High."

Psalm 48:10—"According to Your name, O God, so is Your praise to the ends of the earth; Your right hand is full of righteousness."

Psalm 54:6—"I will freely sacrifice to You; I will praise Your name, O Lord, for it is good."

Psalm 99:3—"Let them praise Your great and awesome name—He is holy."

David knew that it was important to praise God. Praising God all of the time helped David remember God's greatness when he was faced with difficult times. David continually reminded himself who God was and that he had a refuge in God.

One of the best known scriptures for a powerful offering of praise is Acts 16:25. In Acts 16, Paul and Silas were beaten and jailed for casting a demon out of the woman who practiced divination. I am sure that most of us would be thinking that we missed God's calling if we were beaten and jailed. Paul and Silas apparently didn't think this because verse 25 says: "But at midnight Paul and Silas were praying and singing hymns to God, and the prisoners were listening to them."

The situation for Paul and Silas was very serious. They had no idea what their captors had in mind for them. I am sure that they could have been facing a death penalty. With all of this possibly going through their minds, they still prayed and sang praises to God. They knew that God had called them to Macedonia. They knew that they were doing what God had called them to do. They also knew that this battle was not theirs to fight. Their only option was to continue working for God. At midnight they offered themselves, possibly for the last time. They prayed and sang praises. The verse says that the other prisoners were listening to them. Verse 26 says that God also heard them and answered. An earthquake shook the foundations of the prison and opened every door. No prisoner escaped and the jailer immediately gave his heart to God.

Although it is not likely that we would be beaten and go to jail for doing the will of God, we will have trials. (However, let's not be so arrogant to think that we won't be beaten or jailed. Christians are quickly heading into greater persecution around the world).

When we go through our trials, what do we do? Do we get angry? Do we fall apart and throw a pity party? Do we cry out to God and proclaim that it's not fair? Do we think that God has left us on our own? Or do we offer praises for His tender mercies. Do we offer praises because His name is Holy? Do we offer praises because our righteousness comes only from Him?

The group Casting Crowns has a song out called Praise You in This Storm. The whole song is a good reminder that God will never leave us or forsake us.

The part that really strikes home with me is when he wrote, "for You are who You are, no matter where I am." This statement offers praise to God no matter the circumstance. The writer understood that praise for who God is should not be dependent on His provision or our circumstances. It has never been said that everything would be easy when serving God—quite the contrary. We will have plenty of times when we seem to be indestructible Christians. It is as if everything we touch becomes a blessing. There will also be those times when our problems seem to run us over. With that said, God offers His assurance that He is in control. I know that there are times when we don't feel loved by Him or see his hand working on our behalf, but God is in control.

There is another song written by Babbie Mason called Trust His Heart. The song speaks of the difficulty when we are going through a hard time and we can't see God. This song is also a reminder that God has not left us hanging by ourselves.

I am gripped by the words, "When you don't see His plan; when you can't trace His hand; Trust His heart."

King David, Paul and Silas, and a whole host of others trusted the heart of God. They understood the heart of God and how He always came through. The patriarchs of the Bible knew how to offer up heartfelt praises to God. They saw the hand of God move many times on their behalf, but did not limit His praises to His provision.

We must always remember to offer up praises to God for anything and everything. We must live in a state of thankfulness. Yes, be thankful for how and what God provides, but start getting into the habit of praising God just for being God. Praise Him because He is holy. Praise Him because He is worthy of our praise. Praise Him for His sacrifice. Praise Him for His mercy. Praise Him for He is good. Praise Him for His love. Praise Him for His grace. Praise Him because He is righteous. Praise Him for His name's sake. Praise Him for the strength of His right hand. Praise Him just because.

WORSHIP

Worship is probably the hardest of the weapons to define. Why? So far, we have discussed the Word of God, the name of Jesus, obedience, faith, love, forgiveness, prayer, fasting, and praise. You would have a hard time convincing me that I have not already been writing about worship. Every one of these weapons, and the upcoming weapons, are a form of worship to God. Every one of them is required to worship our Father in heaven.

Worship is not isolated to singing a few songs on Sunday morning. Worship is an attitude. It is an attitude of submission to God. Yet it cannot be simply defined as submission. Submission to God is only a form of worship. It is, however, one of the main ingredients. You could also define it as "Face Time with God." God desires that we worship Him. In the Old Testament, the Hebrews became more about where they worshiped than who they worshiped. But, in their defense, they worshiped. At every victorious milestone, they would build a pillar that represented the twelve tribes of Israel and would worship God. They would also name the place to represent how God had provided the victory. I believe that this is one thing that we as believers sincerely fall short in—worship of God. We do not chart the times of victorious moments with God. Why would this be important? As I stated in the last chapter, offering praise (building a pillar) to God acts as a catalyst for your own faith, but also the faith of others. It is a marker for others to see that God is still working on our behalf. As we build those pillars, we need to remember them because there may be a time in the desert when we cannot see God working. If we can walk by the pillar and remember what God had done, it will be much easier to continue our walk.

Again, worship is an attitude. When we see that someone has an attitude, we usually think that they have a problem. But, if we do not have an attitude of worship we have a serious problem.

When we go to church on Sunday, what is our attitude or motivation? Are we going there to socialize, or are we going there to worship God? Are we going there because we think that it is our obligation to the church? Or are we going there because we love God? When we get there, do we not sing because we don't like the music? Or do we sing whether we know the songs or not? Do we listen to the message or ignore the pastor because we are bored? The questions being asked are pointed in opposite directions. One direction is pointed at us and the other is pointed toward God. If our answers point to us, we will never be satisfied in any area of our lives. We will never be satisfied at any church with which we attend. If our answers point toward God and pleasing Him, He will satisfy in the way that Jesus explained to the Samaritan woman. He said in John 4:14, "But whoever drinks of the water that I shall give him will never thirst. But the water that I shall give him will become in him a fountain of water springing up into everlasting life." When we worship God, only He can satisfy our soul.

As we enter into an attitude of worship, it will infiltrate every part of our lives. When things are going very well for us, worship is easy. When life starts getting tough, so does worship. But in order for worship to be a true weapon of our warfare, we need to think of worship in this manner. When the busyness of life makes it difficult to press through in worship of God, worship needs to become our war ship. Our military has several ships of war including the destroyer, aircraft carrier, the battleship, and the submarine. Each vessel has its own purpose and types of missions, but each one fights for a common goal: destroy the works of the enemy. When we see the need to worship God, there is usually a specific thing that tugs at our hearts. It could be personal, or it could be for the needs of others. Nonetheless, our worship to God will put us into battle with our enemy, who is the devil. The person that cut us off in traffic, our friend who offended us, the person who skipped in line at the bank—they are not our enemy. It is up to us to bring our flesh into subjection and worship God. This could be done in the form of forgiving someone, praying for someone, giving food to someone, or giving someone a ride to the store. These acts of worship to God show people that they are important and God has an exalted place in our lives.

When Jesus was tempted in the wilderness He used the Word of God to overcome the enemy. He was worshiping God. When Shadrach, Meshach, Abednego, and Daniel refused to bow to someone or something other than God, they were worshiping God. Their worship became a war ship, captained by God Himself, that destroyed the work of the enemy. When my wife and I refused to allow a premature delivery and death of twin girls destroy our hope for a family, our relationship with each other, and our faith in the Lord, our worship of God carried us through the difficult times. The victory of that time has become a pillar for us, and we use it, often, to minister to others. God has done tremendous things for us and through us since the death of our girls. Has the pain of the loss left us completely? No. But, when we see God use us and the premature delivery to minister to others for His kingdom's sake, we are able to rejoice. We are able to be comforted by His Holy Spirit and know that this event in our lives did not happen in vain.

When tragedy strikes, worship God and see where He takes you. When you can get beyond your own hurt and worship God, He will multiply blessings beyond your wildest dreams. Paul and Silas could not have imagined that their beatings and jail time would lead a man and his family to a saving knowledge of God through Jesus Christ.

Jesus said in John 4:20-24 that worship is not about a certain place to worship God but a place from which we worship God. He said in verse 24: "God is Spirit, and those who worship Him must worship him in spirit and in truth." This true worship comes from deep within the heart of man. It does not matter where you are physically. You could put it this way, it does not matter what state you are in, but the state that your heart is in. One is a location and the other is an attitude. True worship allows us to get beyond ourselves and everything around us. At this point, we can focus totally on the Lord. When we go to church on Sunday, can we forget that there is a multitude surrounding us? Can we focus our hearts on the Lord as if no one else is watching? Can we sing to the Lord as if no one else will hear us? Can we dance before the Lord as if no one else is around? Sadly, most of us would have to say no. Me included. Worship is one on one with God. It does not seek attention. It does not seek any glory that is due to God alone. Worship is not puffed up. Worship is first selfless to God and His kingdom desires. Worship desires to exhort others into a closer relationship to God. One might ask why it is so important to go to church if there are a lot of distractions to our worship. Please remember that true worship of God happens any day of the week and anywhere we are, but we should never forsake being assembled together with other believers (Hebrews 10:25). We should also not let others intimidate us from really worshipping God because of what they might think. God is the object of our worship, not the other people. If everyone would radically worship God, the strength of our corporate, unified worship would be a deafening blow to the enemy.

One very special note about worship; God will not share our worship with anyone or anything. God is jealous of our worship. He will not intrude on our free will, but has made it clear that He desires us to be clean before Him. He desires for us to fellowship with Him; thus, the reason that the veil was torn in two. We have been made worthy to enter His presence by His own Son, Jesus. Always remember, when we get into worshiping other people or things, they will be changing their rules every day. God is the same yesterday, today, and forever. Serving God is much easier than serving others. True worship is being a true servant of God. His rules do not change because He does not change.

TESTIMONY

Imagine yourself in a court of law as the accused. You are waiting for the first witness to be sworn in and begin to answer the attorneys' questions. You are nervous because you have no idea what this particular witness did or did not see. You believe that your attorney had built a pretty solid case for your defense, but you don't know what information the prosecuting attorney has. You are at the mercy of the court. The witness has been sworn in and has been asked the first question. You can hardly breathe.

The prosecuting attorney asks the witness, "What did you see on the night of the crime?"

"I saw that man commit the crime in question."

Wow, eye witness testimony against you. It can be very condemning. Your life hangs in the balance with every word. It is a powerful tool used by the court system to make sure that the accused are either put behind bars or set free if the evidence does not match the testimony.

Our testimony is not just powerful in a court of law. It is a powerful weapon of our warfare. We are to use our testimony to speak of the many good things that God has done to bring victory in our lives. It is a way of sharing the gospel of Jesus. It may be the one thing that helps someone believe in Jesus.

The problem with most believers today is this, we have gotten used to having everything come to us quickly. We have a hard time waiting two minutes for the microwave to warm up the leftovers. We can't sit at a traffic light without grumbling. We hate it when we have a 1:00 p.m. doctor's appointment and we are still in the waiting room at 1:30. All of these situations allow us the opportunity to tell the world about our problems. This has become our testimony. I have heard stories about friends of complainers who hide behind things at the store to avoid being seen by the complainers. They know that if they are seen, they will be there for a long time, listening to their problems. You would think that the word testimony was pronounced "Test and moaning."

It is true that there are a lot of problems in this world. We do have bad days. We do have financial problems. We do have arguments with our friends. And it is hard not to complain about them. We must, however, remember the testimony of God:

> Deuteronomy 28:13- "And the Lord will make you the head and not the tail; you shall be above only, and not be beneath, if you heed the commandments of the Lord your God, which I command you today, and are careful to observe them.

> Deuteronomy 33:12–"The beloved of the Lord shall dwell in safety by Him, Who shelters him

all the day long; And he shall dwell between His shoulders."

Psalm 57:3–"He shall send from heaven and save me; He reproaches the one who would swallow me up. Selah God shall send forth His mercy and His truth."

Jeremiah 29:11–"For I know the thoughts that I think toward you, says the Lord, thoughts of peace and not of evil, to give you a future and a hope."

John 15:16–"You did not choose me, but I chose you and appointed you that you should go and bear fruit, and that your fruit should remain, that whatever you ask the Father in my name He may give you."

It says in 2 Corinthians 6:18–"I will be a Father to you, And you shall be my sons and daughters, Says the Lord Almighty."

I know that I barely scratched the surface with scriptures of what God thinks of us, but I think that you should get the point. God's Word is just as powerful in these scriptures as in Genesis, when He created everything. His passion for us has never diminished, and it will never end. His testimony over us is love, grace, mercy, tenderness, and all good things. When we struggle, though, we blame God for our circumstance. Is it His fault? Examine your situation. Have you walked out from under His covering? He is a strong tower to which we should be running. We can take comfort under the shadow of His wings. With Him, there is protection.

It is very important that our testimony match that of our Father. We should always remind ourselves of who we are in Him. A pastor of mine once said; "Jesus died on the cross for you, how bad can it really be?"

Isaiah 54:17 says, "No weapon formed against you shall prosper, and every tongue which rises against you in judgment You shall condemn. This is the heritage of the servants of the Lord, and their righteousness is from me, says the Lord."

It says that there is not a weapon formed that can destroy you. It also says that you will condemn every tongue that tries to bring judgment against you. The only stipulation to this is staying under the covering of God.

Billy Graham is an excellent example of this. If a woman tried to accuse him of sexual harassment, he could rest under the shadow of God's wings. Why? Billy Graham would not place himself in a situation where he would be alone with a woman. He refuses to open that door of temptation. If he is waiting for an elevator and a woman is on there alone, he would let it go and wait for the next one. He does not want his testimony for God to be damaged by his carelessness. He also does not want his flesh to be tempted. God has honored the ministry of Billy Graham because of his faithfulness.

Before Jesus was put on trial, Peter said that he would never deny Him and that he would die for Jesus. That was a pretty powerful testimony. But when the test came, he did a lot of moaning. He refused to tell the truth. He said that he did not know Jesus. When the rooster crowed in the morning, Peter recalled his conversation with Jesus and was ashamed. Why was Peter so ashamed of his testimony? The people who asked him if he was a follower of Jesus may have suspected this but did not really know. The fact is, Peter knew what he had said. Even at this point, Peter did not fully understand Jesus when He said that He would rise on the third day. Peter may have had a hint that Jesus would be executed, but even if He was, Peter's testimony would have gone to Jesus' grave. That is how powerful our testimonies are. Most people don't have a hard time selling the other guy out to save their own skin, and that is why we are overcome with guilt. When our testimony does not line up with the truth, we place things out of order with how they are supposed to be.

Let's go back to the courtroom. The prosecuting attorney has brought about some pretty powerful evidence against you. The testimony of his witness was very convincing to the jury. The judge himself could not deny the facts set before him, yet he has to await the verdict of the jury. As the jury deliberates, you agonize about the outcome. You know that things are not looking good, but your attorney has an excellent record in this courtroom. When the jury re-enters the courtroom to announce their verdict, everyone awaits with anticipation. The judge asks the foreman if they have reached a verdict and the foremen affirms that they have. The Jury foreman pronounces "Guilty on all counts." The prosecutors are elated and you are sobbing. The courtroom erupts with a lot of commotion. The judge orders everyone to be quiet as your attorney approaches the bench. After a few moments with the judge, the judge orders your release at the protest of the prosecuting attorney. He pronounces that your advocate has taken your place, and it is His testimony about His love for you that has made you free. Our advocate is Jesus Christ, and He has paid our sin debt. His truth is His sinless testimony before His Father. John 8:32 says, "You shall know the truth, and the truth shall make you free." Revelation 12:11, "And they overcame him by the blood of the Lamb and by the word of their testimony, and they did not love their lives to the death." The blood of the lamb has already paid the price for your freedom, but your testimony will keep you free. Your testimony brings victory if the Word of God is the fountain from which it comes.

HUMILITY

There is a scene played out that is very real in the lives of many people. Someone gets fixated on an individual because they see them from a glamorous viewpoint and believe that the person is like that all of the time. They imagine what it would be like to live in their shoes or be in their circle of friends. They have dreams of meeting their fixation. If their dream does come true, it is usually met with great disappointment because their fixation is not what was imagined. Most come away feeling dejected because they were treated poorly and made to feel like they were not important and intruding in the space of the glamour. As a child growing up there was an individual who was a superstar in my eyes. He was a pillar of the community and did many wonderful things. I knew early on that he did have a bit of a foul mouth but overlooked that due to his good deeds and stardom. In my early adult years, I had the opportunity to see this man in a video that was less than pleasant. In this video were outtakes of him using vile profanity. His use of profanity was not just a few words here and there, but very extreme and often. At that moment I knew that I had a distorted view of him and finally had the opportunity to see him as he really was. My view was never the same. This happens at all levels of society when anyone is placed on a pedestal; they will eventually make a mistake in the eyes of the one who put them there and be unceremoniously removed.

Most of the disappointment starts with someone seeing your pride. Most of us can recognize the pride of another person but can't see our own pride. Pride is the complete opposite of humility. Pride is the source of all who fall from power. There have been many ministries consumed by pride. Pride is one thing that God detests.

I know that I am supposed to be writing about humility, but pride is what rages against it so easily. Pride is what undermines the foundations of humility. I will have to say here that we should be very careful not to have our testimony steal any glory from God. God is jealous and will not share His glory with anyone. Be careful of those whose testimonies are proclamations of their works for God. It is great to tell about ministry opportunities that God has given us, but do not shine the light on yourselves. It is God who has called us and God who works in and through us. And to God goes all of the glory, honor, and praise. Proverbs 27:2 says, "Let another man praise you, and not your own mouth; A stranger, and not your own lips." James 4:6 and 1 Peter 5:5 state, "God resists the proud and gives grace to the humble."

There are many other scriptures that declare God's opinion of pride but I believe that you get the picture.

We could all make a more concerted effort at humility. Humility is very hard to walk in and very easy to lose. But, as a weapon of warfare, it shatters every high thing that exalts itself against the knowledge of God. When we have something that comes against us, how do we react? Do our feelings get hurt, or do we pray for those who despitefully use us? When we think that we should get a promotion but someone else gets it, do we get angry or congratulate the other person? When someone has become the star athlete, do we get jealous or do we work that much harder to improve our game? When someone gets the invitation to minister and you feel that God has given you a message to preach, do you refuse to support that individual or do you pray that God ignites a fire of anointing in them?

I could go on with many other examples, but I have already written many of my own weaknesses for you to read. I have suffered many bouts with pride only to realize that God has always been with me. When we walk in humility, we are refusing to give place to the enemy. When we walk in humility, we are walking in the Spirit of God. Galatians 5:16 says, "Walk in the Spirit, and you shall not fulfill the lust of the flesh." The rest of the chapter goes on to define the works of the flesh in verses 19-21. In my Bible I have subtitled it "Rebellion defined." In verses 22-26, the Word of God explains the fruit of the Spirit which I subtitled as "Holiness defined." When we walk in humility, we fulfill the law of God—verse 18. When we walk after the flesh, we will not inherit the kingdom of God—verse 21.

I cannot write this chapter with the idea that walking in humility is easy. It is probably the hardest thing for a Christian to do. There are so many things that can cause us to forget about humility. When a person offends us, it is easy for our pride to swell within us. When someone sings our praises for a job well done, it is easy for us to swell with pride. When we make a mistake, it is so easy for us to become defensive and try to throw blame in another direction.

With that said, there are also a lot of opportunities for us to walk in humility. If you are working on a project with another person, and they have done at least half of the work, humility shares the credit. Even if you are the star athlete, humility shares credit with the other teammates. If you make a mistake, humility makes an admission of guilt and faces the consequences. If you are sitting on a bus and a woman with a child gets on, humility offers her the seat. If someone hurts you, humility forgives. If someone hates you, humility loves anyway. If someone is angry with you, humility offers gentleness in return.

Again, none of this is easy to walk in, but it is essential if we are to show the world that Jesus is a life changer. If we are to tell people that God loves them, we are to walk in love. If we are to show the world that God is forgiving, we are to walk in forgiveness. If we walk in humility with the purpose of giving God the glory, we become true lights of the Gospel of Christ.

Let me give you one final warning. Do not walk in false humility. There are many that struggle with this phrase, but I believe that it's real. Let me give you a scriptural reference. In Luke 18:11 we have the story of the publican and the Pharisee. The Pharisee, in his attempt to show God how humble he was, declared his goodness over others to God. He said this: "God, I thank you that I am not like other men—extortioners, unjust, adulterers, or even as this tax collector. I fast twice a week; I give tithes of all that I possess." I really don't think that God needed the Pharisee to tell Him his good deeds and godly exploits. How often do we compare ourselves to others? How often do we share how well we are working for God? How often do we tell others how much we give to the poor? How often do we belittle our efforts to others when we are actually fishing for compliments?

The publican, on the other hand, said this, "God, be merciful to me, a sinner!" He knew that there was nothing good inside him. He knew that he had nothing to compare to anyone else. He knew that grace only comes from God. He knew that God was his source. Jesus said that the publican went home justified.

False humility is just another form of pride. It is a blind allusion that reeks with the odor of sin. However, true humility brings glory to God. When we walk in true humility, others will benefit. True humility raises others to new levels.

I now exhort you to study the scriptures. I pray that I have brought out the truth of God to you and raised your desire to walk in His fullness. Jesus is our ultimate example in all aspects of life and ministry. He loved without measure. He took no credit for Himself but desired that all of the people knew more about God. Even when His fame went abroad, His greatest desire was to declare the kingdom of God rather than receive the praise of men. His humility was contagious. After the Holy Spirit was given, the apostles were very clear that they were not the ones who healed people. They said that it was Jesus who was doing the work through them. So, too, are we to walk in this manner. Jesus said in the book of John, several times, that He was doing what He saw His Father doing, or He was doing what His Father told Him to do. In all of these instances, He was giving all glory to God. Jesus could have easily taken credit for the work that He was doing but chose to give it away. We have authority given to us to use the name of Jesus and His Word; however, we have no authority to receive any credit for the work that God has called us to. Too many ministers have fallen from high places because of pride. Even if we are not in a high place, pride will make the fall seem as if we have fallen from a mountaintop. Walk in humility because it is as close to God as we can get.

JOY

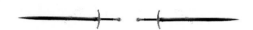

"For though we walk in the flesh, we do not war according to the flesh: For the weapons of our warfare are not carnal, but mighty through God to the pulling down of strong holds" (2 Corinthians 10:3-4).

When God created us in His own image, He had in mind a created being that would exemplify all of heaven and who He is. He wanted us to be a human example of Himself. With that said, we obviously can't go creating animals, planets, and other living things with our words. God is the only one that can create life and set all things in order. We were created in His image by having a body, soul, and spirit. We are a three-part being just as God is three parts, but one equal God. Where things fell apart for us was in the garden of Eden. Adam and Eve were tricked into believing that a moment of happiness would replace the joy of God's presence. We fight these same battles today.

There is a great deal of confusion about the difference between happiness and joy. We also have the same reality checks that Adam had when we substitute a temporary fix of happiness in place of joy. There is one major difference between happiness and joy. Please leave with this understanding—Things that make us happy have strings attached to them. Here is an example of what I am talking about. If you were to buy a new flat screen TV, you would probably be fairly happy. After getting the TV home, you would have to have some sort of cable programming to get the most out of your purchase. Once you have the TV and the cable programming, you would have to pay the monthly expense of the cable. Now you need a job that will cover that expense. In order to get to your job, you would have to get a car. You would probably have to get a loan to pay for the car so you would try to work extra hours for the extra income. All of the extra hours at work minimize the time that you get to watch the TV you just bought. The moment of happiness had so many strings attached that it eventually became a web of deception. The same web that ensnared Adam and Eve.

Joy, on the other hand, can be explained in this way. It only comes from God. That pretty much settles the debate, but I will continue with my explanation. Joy does not have any strings attached. Since God is the perfect gentleman, He will not infringe His will over yours; however, He does have a plan for you. He has promised His goodness over you and He will not forget those promises. True joy is embodied in the act of service. Don't make a mistake in thinking that works will bring us joy. It is not by works, it is by service. There is a difference. Works go after the praise of men and service seeks no reward. When we act with a servant's heart, the joy comes when we are not looking for a return on the investment.

When someone has a works mentality, they want an immediate reward. A person that has a servant's heart understands that his reward may not come immediately but realizes that being a blessing to others is an immediate reward.

When we read about anything to do with the Bible, we should always look to Jesus as our ultimate example. Jesus Christ was more than a prophet. He lived exactly how He wants us to live. In all things He displayed joy. And I can imagine that you are thinking about the time He turned the money changers' tables over. You are correct in thinking that He displayed anger. He did, but I will say that He displayed joy toward His Father. It was the joy of His Father that caused Him to set things right in the temple. As in all things though, He was led by the Holy Spirit. Even Jesus would have refrained in the temple if the Holy Spirit had told Him.

In John 15:10-12, Jesus is explaining who He is in the Father and who we are in Him. "If you keep My commandments, you will abide in My love, just as I have kept My Father's commandments and abide in His love. These things I have spoken to you, that My joy may remain in you, and that your joy may be full."

If we want to live a life of joy, His joy, we are to keep His commandments. That sounds pretty easy doesn't it? Well, let's see what verse 12 says: "This is my commandment, that you love one another as I have loved you." If you will remember, the two greatest commandments are these: "You shall love the Lord your God with all your heart, with all your soul, with all your strength, and with all your mind, and your neighbor as yourself" (Luke 10:27). If we live the law of love, as He commanded, His joy will remain in us and our joy (which comes from Jesus) will be full. With Jesus being our example, He never wavered in His love toward Judas. If we were in His position, knowing that Judas would betray us, we would not have washed his feet.

The Lord showed me something about personal relationships many years ago. He said, "Your relationship with another person depends only on you." What He meant was that it should not matter how another person treats me for me to show them love or treat them well. If we can get beyond the face value of how someone treats us, we will have joy in the Lord. We will be fulfilling the scripture, "The joy of the Lord is our strength" (Nehemiah 8:10). I, personally, have people in my life that grate on my nerves, and it takes a lot of effort to get beyond my feelings. When I trust God, and rest in His strength, His joy is fulfilled in my life. I can enjoy their company when I submit to God and show them love.

I used to be a person that did not enjoy the company of a lot of people. When my wife and I had groups of people at our house, I would end up hiding in our room. Something would irritate me, I would hide, and she had to cover for me. I was a person who did not have a lot of joy in my life. It has only been in the last couple of years that I have had a release. I have been relying on God to help me show love toward others and I have had my joy made full. I feel like a person that is being completed in Christ.

When we operate with joy in our lives, we are disrupting the work of our enemy, the devil. His greatest desire is to steal, kill, and destroy everything positive in our lives. He wants us angry, unhappy, and dissolved of any hope. When we have joy in our lives, we can put those things to rest. It does not mean that we are without our personal struggles. It is, however, as if we are letting our weaknesses rest on the strength of the Lord. With the joy of the Father in our hearts, love comes easier and our faith seems stronger.

It is hard to imagine how horrible the cross was for Jesus to endure. Who can accurately give a descriptive account of the events surrounding that day? Mel Gibson's movie, The Passion of the Christ, is probably the closest to giving a visual reference, but it still probably fell short of the truth. But when I read Hebrews 12:2, I am in awe that Jesus saw His joy beyond the cross. The scripture states: "Looking unto Jesus, the author and finisher of our faith, who for the joy that was set before Him endured the cross, despising the shame, and has sat down at the right hand of the throne of God." I believe that Jesus could endure the cross because of the joy He would have in welcoming His bride into His glory. His sorrow and agony was a fleeting moment compared to eternity with His bride.

Please remember that we can be happy and be without joy. If we try to fill our lives with stuff, we will only have momentary glimpses of happiness, stuffed with large quantities of being unfulfilled. If we become servants of the Lord and begin walking in our calling, we will have our joy made complete in Him. Our first calling is to love God and the second is to love others. Perfect joy is made complete with love. Perfect love is made complete when we walk with a servant's heart.

Our faith in God works by the love of Christ emanating from our hearts. Walk in love and live in joy.

PEACE

Let's play a game. The game where I mention a word and you say the first thing that comes to your mind. Are you read? Let's go! The word is peace.

I am certain that the answers would be as varying as there are copies of this book. As I began to meditate on this word, I also thought of different types of peace. Some of the definitions for peace are as follows: An absence of war; an agreement or treaty to end hostilities; freedom from quarrels and disagreement; harmonious relations; inner contentment and serenity. Many of you probably thought of these same things for your answers, but allow me to throw a wrench in everything that you know about peace.

Peace is a weapon of spiritual warfare! Oh, it is true that two people or nations can live together in peace even if they do not agree on everything. And a peace treaty is an agreement between two nations not to attack one another or their mutual friends. However, peace treaties are only good between the nations that sign them. The people of each nation can rest pretty easily by having the understanding that the other nation of the treaty will not do anything to harm them. What about the other countries that don't like your nation?

There are a lot of countries and people that still do not have much international peace since the attacks on 9/11. So where does peace come from? It certainly does not come from the worldly systems. Our governments are mostly corrupt, the financial systems are bankrupt, our medical systems are incredible, but also incredibly self-absorbed. Every known "manmade" system that we rely on cannot provide any lasting peace. So where does peace come from? There is only one place and He is our Prince of Peace—Jesus.

When Jesus was born the angels declared in Luke 2:14, "Glory to God in the highest, and on earth peace and good will toward men." We still use this phrase at Christmastime. It is desirable to have peace on earth and wish goodwill toward others, but we need to understand the role of the church in this message. Let's take a look at two scriptures. Mark 9:50 and Luke 12:51 appear to have two different meanings about the word peace, yet Jesus said both of them. Mark 9:50, "Salt is good, but if the salt loses its flavor, how will you season it? Have salt in yourselves, and have peace with one another." Luke 12:51, "Do you suppose that I came to give peace on earth? I tell you, not at all, but rather division."

How can this be so? How can we be told to live at peace with each other and Jesus said that He did not come to bring peace? Please remember what Jesus said in John 3:16-17,

> For God so loved the world that He gave His only begotten Son, that whoever believes in Him should not perish but have everlasting life.

For God did not send His Son into the world to condemn the world, but that the world through Him might be saved.

God's desire is that everyone would come to a saving knowledge of Him through Jesus.

However, there are those that are completely blinded by the enemy and will never see the truth. With them there will not be peace. In Mark 9:50, we are called to be the salt of the earth. We are to be the flavor of God wherever we are. My pastor has talked about being marinated with God's presence so that we are the flavor of God. If we have the flavor of God, we can change the atmosphere around us and be an offering of peace. We can be the rainbow in a dark storm. If we walk in the joy of the Lord, we can cause others to ask us why we have hope. But please don't be confused by Luke 12:51. Jesus was not referring to natural peace. Everything in the natural is controlled from the spiritual. I am not saying that we are pawns in a chess match, but we have choices to make every day and those choices are derived from the spiritual. When we do good things and make the right decisions, they come from God. When we do bad things and make bad choices, they come from Satan. In Luke 12:51 Jesus is not saying there is no hope for peace, but knowing that Satan is going about to kill, steal, and destroy all that he can deceive, there won't be peace between the two spiritual realms.

The desire that Jesus has is for His church to understand that His peace is more than enough to survive this world. As believers, we are to hold onto the promises of God and live as if God really did win the war for our lives. It is also our job to share this victory with others. We must also take a stand. There are so many things that the world is trying to do to influence how the church is to operate. Being at peace does not mean that we should compromise the Word of God. We cannot bow down to the world's demands. In Matthew 21:12-14, Jesus cleansed the temple of those that were being influenced by the world. He declared that His Father's house is a house of prayer and that they had made it a den of thieves. If we allow the world to run our churches, they will become a place empty of God's presence. We are to show everyone around us that God is the only way to true peace.

During the Vietnam War there was a peace movement that swept across the United States. Many of the people were saying, "We want peace and not war." We are still reeling from that movement today. There is a call for peace without a true understanding of its cost. They want peace by talking to those who hate us. They want peace by having everyone destroy all of their weapons; when, in fact, only the honest ones would. What these people are looking for is some kind of utopia that does not exist. As believers, we can offer the only peace that truly exists. We must offer the Prince of Peace. Our peace came with a high price. Jesus offered Himself as the one sacrifice to give us peace. He did not offer a utopian experience but provided a lasting peace if we follow His Word.

Jesus said in John 14:27, "Peace I leave with you, my peace I give to you; not as the world gives do I give to you. Let not your heart be troubled, neither let it be afraid."

What kind of peace does the world offer? The world would have us believe that true peace comes from a survivalist attitude—meaning that only the strong will survive. The world would tell us that financial freedom will give us peace, but you can look at the torment of those that don't have financial struggles and see that this is a lie. The world would tell a young woman that an unplanned pregnancy will keep her from fulfilling her dreams. They tell her that an abortion will bring peace from a bad decision. Most of these young women have found that the abortion did not bring the peace that was promised. Many ended up committing suicide as a result of their abortion torment. I could go on and on about the false peace of the world, but will say only this; we need to look at the times that we sought peace from the world and remember how many times that it only brought disappointment.

What kind of peace does Jesus have to offer? I will start with Luke 10:17-20. In this set of verses the seventy disciples that Jesus had sent out returned from their assignments. They were excited that "even the devils were subject" to them through the name of Jesus. Jesus answered them with this in verse 20, "Nevertheless do not rejoice in this, that the spirits are subject to you, but rather rejoice because your names are written in heaven." I am sure that the disciples were very excited about their trip, but Jesus was trying to give them a warning. There are times when we feel like we can walk on water, and then have times of complete failure. Our peace does not rest in those times of victory, but that we are going to be in heaven with Him. We need to recount victories in our lives to be reminded of God working, but there will be another battle tomorrow.

Let me give you one final word when comparing peace from this world and the peace from Jesus. I won't deny that we all have struggles with peace in our hearts, but let's examine why we don't have peace. Where do we tie up our finances? Where do we tie up our time? Those two questions can probably answer most of our peace problems. Start seeking the Lord for help in redirecting those to areas of our lives that should bring Him more glory and honor and allow us to live in His peace. Galatians 5:22 says that peace is a fruit of the spirit of God. True peace can only come from God because it is a part of who He is. True peace originates from God and can only be operated from an impartation of His Spirit. It is a peace without compromise. It is a peace that brings glory to God alone.

In Daniel 3:17-18 (KJV), Shadrach, Meshach, and Abednego told this to King Nebuchadnezzar before being taken to the fiery furnace:

> If it be so, our God whom we serve is able to deliver us from the burning fiery furnace, and He will deliver us out of your hand, O king. But, if not, be it known unto thee, O king, that we will not serve your gods, nor worship the golden image which you have set up.

Wow, what boldness. What faith. What peace. The king was offering them peace if they would only bow to the golden image; they knew that this would only be a short-lived peace. They knew that they had to answer to God and that He offered the only true peace. We need to have the attitude of Shadrach, Meshach, and Abednego.

To close, I want to list some scriptures that will encourage us all in knowing Jesus as our Prince of Peace.

Isaiah 26:3–"You will keep him in perfect peace, whose mind is stayed on You, because he trusts in You."

Philippians 4:6-7–"Be anxious for nothing, but in everything by prayer and supplication, with thanksgiving, let your requests be made known to God; and the peace of God, which surpasses all understanding, will guard your hearts and minds through Christ Jesus."

John 14:27–"Peace I leave with you, my peace I give to you; not as the world gives do I give to you. Let not your heart be troubled, neither let it be afraid."

John 16:33–"These things I have spoken to you, that in me you may have peace. In the world you will have tribulation; but be of good cheer, I have overcome the world."

Colossians 3:15–"And let the peace of God rule in your hearts, to which also you were called in one body; and be thankful."

2 Thessalonians 3:16–"Now the Lord of peace Himself will give you peace always by all means. The Lord be with you."

2 Corinthians 13:11–"Finally, brethren, farewell. Be perfect, be of good comfort, be of one mind, live in peace; and the God of love and peace will be with you."

May the peace of God surround you in all things.

LONGSUFFERING

I sincerely pray that each of you have been blessed by this book, but I must say that each chapter seems to be getting tougher to write. Each weapon seems as if it is harder to live through. I am beginning to realize that most, if not all, writers for God can't possibly have it all together. I have been writing about having victory in our lives by utilizing the weapons that God designed for us to overcome the enemy; however, I am finding them difficult to use most of the time. Yes, this is a bit of a confession, but also a profession. I/we will overcome the enemy because the victory has been won. I believe the reason for my own testing has been to help me write about the weapons of warfare. I have had some serious questions for God about a few particular things and the waiting has been very difficult. When the Word says that longsuffering is a fruit of the Spirit, I don't believe that we can fully comprehend its meaning without some longsuffering. This is not an easy journey.

I looked on the Internet about longsuffering and found that a lot of people relate it to patience. While I won't disagree with them, I wanted to share with you one thought that really struck a chord with me. Please read the next statement very carefully—Longsuffering can also be referred to as patience. Patience is being mild, gentle, and constant in all circumstances. The real test of patience is not in waiting, but in how one acts while he or she is waiting (www.christcenteredmall. com).

Did you catch that? It said the real test of patience is not in waiting, but in how we act while we are waiting. Wow, that really says a lot. After reading this statement I realized that I was a long way from reflecting Christ with my waiting. I had some struggles in a job position at an employer, and while focusing on my problems I made it difficult for others see a true reflection of Christ in me. I developed some anger issues from the problems, and that hindered my witness for Christ. I have since had a tremendous turnaround and the anger has passed.

Longsuffering is not an impossible task. If it were, God would show Himself to be unmerciful. Let's take a look at a few scriptures concerning the longsuffering of God.

> Exodus 34:6–"And the Lord passed before him and proclaimed, 'The Lord, the Lord God, merciful and gracious, longsuffering, and abounding in goodness and truth … '"

> Numbers 14:18–"The Lord is longsuffering and abundant in mercy, forgiving iniquity and transgression; but He by no means clears the guilty, visiting the iniquity of the fathers on the children to the third and fourth generation."

Psalm 86:15–"But You, O Lord, are a God full of compassion, and gracious, longsuffering and abundant in mercy and truth."

2 Peter 3:9–"The Lord is not slack concerning His promise, as some count slackness, but is longsuffering toward us, not willing that any should perish but that all should come to repentance."

2 Peter 3:15–" ... and consider that the longsuffering of our Lord is salvation."

It is by God's longsuffering that we can be saved from a punishment that we truly deserve. We know that the grace we received from God means unmerited favor. Throughout the scriptures it says that God is slow to anger and full of compassion. God is not willing for anyone to perish but live with Him throughout eternity. This can only happen if we have a relationship with Him through Jesus Christ.

As much as I would like to, I cannot say that I am slow to anger, merciful, full of compassion, ready to pardon, and abundant in kindness. Most people that know me have seen me show a less than Christ like attitude on occasion. I am quite certain that we have all wanted people to forget those moments of rage that we display. We get hotheaded and selfish at times, and we do not walk out our faith. We do not display much longsuffering. I won't say that it's okay to act this way, but we don't need to make ourselves suffer from acts of stupidity. God desires for us to repent and get over it as quickly as possible. Learn from it and move on.

In today's society it is very difficult to wait for anything. We have a generation that always wants the newest thing even if the last newest thing was just released a month ago. We are becoming an indebted society because we just can't wait for anything. Let's take a look in Genesis to learn a little about waiting and what happened when man got in the way.

In Genesis 12, we see that Abram (Abraham) was found to be pleasing in the sight of God. God told him that He would make Abram a great nation. This was God's first promise of children for Abram. God said that He would bless Abram and that Abram would be a blessing. God also told Abram that all families would be blessed because of him. This is yet another promise of children for Abram and his wife. In Genesis 15:5, God showed Abram that his seed would be numbered as the stars of heaven, and Abraham believed Him. This is very important for us to understand, when God makes a promise, He means it. In chapter 16, Abram really missed the boat. He let Sarai talk him into something other than God's promise. They tried to make the promise of God happen through the back door. They could not wait for God to fulfill His promise on His terms. Abram had made Hagar pregnant, which was 180 degrees away from where God wanted Abram and Sarai to be. In Genesis 17:4-5, God once again told Abraham that he would be a father of many nations.

God has made a great display of His longsuffering with Abram (Abraham). Abraham was told several times by God that he would have children yet had to intervene in the promise that was made. You would think that God would have given up on Abraham and chose to use someone else to fulfill the promise of God. That is not how God works. It is God's greatest desire to fulfill His promises in us, even when we mess things up due to our lack of patience/longsuffering. God still wants to bring good to us.

God has a purpose for each one of us and He is not slack in His promises for us. Our problem is that we are a lot like Abraham. We do our best to circumvent the timing of God's promises because we think it is taking too long for them to be fulfilled. This is by no means a condemnation. It is a wakeup call for us all. I have heard many times that God will use someone else if an individual messes up and forsakes the promise or prophecy. With what is written about Abraham, I can see that the statement is false. Although Abraham made plenty of mistakes, God continued to nurture him into the man that God saw from the beginning. In the midst of Abraham's short comings, God continued to tell him that he would be a father to many nations. God never became so disgusted with Abraham that He gave up on him. My friends, God will never give up on you or me either. He wants nothing but the best for us and He will always raise us up to higher levels. His calling for each one of us is personal and His desire is to fulfill each calling for us all.

I remember about fifteen years ago that someone spoke a particular thing over me and I thought she was absolutely off her rocker. She said it this way; "I see you as a _____." I responded in this manner: "Well, I don't see it." At that point it didn't matter if I could see it or not, God was showing her something. My walk with God during those fifteen years was like a rollercoaster. There were times when I felt really close to the Lord, and then times where I walked like I never got saved. Again, it did not matter if I could see how God saw me in the future. All that mattered was God's promise over me. His greatest desire for me is to fulfill my purpose in Him, and He has always been in a position to out wait me. With regard to that vision over me, I still feel like I am a long way from seeing it come to pass, but I can at least begin to see that it could come to pass. This is not something that I desire as a personal goal, but I do desire to please God.

Let's get back to Abraham. Isaac was not born until chapter 21. Ishmael had already been born long before; and Abraham had already made several blundering mistakes. With all of Abraham's problems, God fulfilled His promises to him. How much easier would it have been for Abraham if he had just waited on the Lord? There are many of us that have lives that mirror Abraham's in a lot of ways. Will we continue our faith journey anyway and place ourselves in a position to have God fulfill His purpose for our lives? When Abraham was going through his difficult times, he still found God to be his foundation. He always went back to the source of the covenant. With all that Abraham did to mess things up, God still counted him as a man of faith. That is incredible. God never once gave up on Abraham. God continued to tell him that He had a promise to fulfill in him. The same can be said for you and me. No matter where we are right now, God has commanded His love toward us to complete the good work that He has already begun. I know that waiting is not always the most joyful thing for us to do, but we must.

Remember, when we wait on the Lord, it's not that we are waiting on Him, but how we are waiting. While we are waiting on the Lord, it has to be with graciousness, humility, mercy, and tenderness. I will close with this statement. God is not toying with us like we would dangle a carrot in front of a horse; He is working on us to make us look more like Himself.

KINDNESS

Have you ever heard the phrase "Kill them with kindness?" It really seems kind of odd to think of killing in this way. As I looked this up on the Internet, I found out that the phrase originated in this form—kill with kindness as fond apes do their young (presumably crushing them to death in a hug). It became a proverb of the 1500s. So I can dispel any thoughts that I have lost my marbles, I will make it clear now that I don't actually want you to kill anyone. But, I wish to remind everyone that kindness will go a long way to turn away wrath. Proverbs 15:1 says that a soft answer turns away wrath. Kindness is a main ingredient for a soft answer.

As I have ministered at church before, every believer in Christ has a calling from the Lord to minister to the lost. Second Corinthians 5:17-21 says:

> Therefore, if anyone is in Christ, he is a new creation; old things have passed away; behold, all things have become new. Now all things are of God, who has reconciled us to Himself through Jesus Christ, and has given us the ministry of reconciliation, that is, that God was in Christ reconciling the world to Himself, not imputing their trespasses to them, and has committed to us the word of reconciliation.

Now then, we are ambassadors for Christ, *as though God were pleading through us:* we implore you on Christ's behalf, be reconciled to God. For He made Him who knew no sin to be sin for us, that we might become the righteousness of God in Him.

(emphasis mine)

In this scripture, God reveals His heart toward us by showing that He believes in us to complete His work on the earth. We have been given an awesome responsibility of sharing His love for all people of every nation, tribe, and tongue. I like what the scripture says—"as though God were pleading through us." If God is pleading through us; are we sharing His message as He would? Are we sharing it with love? Does the world see the body of Christ as a body that loves at all costs, or does it see His body painfully reacting to every blow on the chin? Don't get me wrong, the body of Christ has to be bold and stand up for God with righteousness. We can't bow down to the demands of the world. We must live what we preach though. If we preach love and kindness, the world must see love and kindness.

In 1 Corinthians 13:4-8 it says, "Love suffers long and is kind; love does not envy; love does not parade itself, is not puffed up; does not behave rudely, does not seek its own, is not provoked, thinks no evil; does not rejoice in iniquity, but rejoices in the truth; bears all things, believes all things, hopes all things, endures all things. Love never fails."

We are supposed to be changing into the image of God by Jesus Christ, but what is the world seeing?

The scripture in 1 Corinthians is the explicit image of Jesus because it reveals the attributes of Christ that we should portray. When we can put off our old man and live out these scriptures, we will be slaying the heart of our enemy that rules in the emptiness of a soul without Christ. God is not willing that any should perish; are we? If we are to bare the image of God, we must show kindness to all.

I have shared with someone before, "If you want friends, you have to be friendly."

I can't count the times that I missed an opportunity to share the gospel with someone because I was not in the right frame of mind to do so. I did not have the mind of Christ. I used to live in fear of company at our home. I would start off just fine, but after a while I would get overwhelmed and hide in the bedroom. I was not showing the kindness of God that He demanded of me. This wasn't just my struggle either. My wife had to pay a heavy price for my being inconsiderate. When we fall short in our calling, we are not the only ones affected. It affects those closest to us, and the people that God has placed in our path. If we are having a moment of ungraciousness, we will not share the gospel. Or, for that matter, it will not be received.

As a testimony of God's resurrection power, I can now rejoice at having company at our home. I love opening our home for Bible studies. I love having people over for Thanksgiving and any other occasion. It is in these moments that I get to share the love of God through kindness. God has delivered me from my oppression of loneliness and fear. God has been so good to my wife and me and has opened up ministry opportunities through this deliverance.

We are not called to be closet Christians. I am sure that you have heard someone say, "My faith is personal. It is between me and God." Part of this statement is true—it is personal. Meaning that we have to stand on our own faith and we cannot carry anyone else on our faith. The statement is incorrect because it implies that we are not supposed to share our faith. Believers of God, it is our job to exalt the name of God through the gospel of Jesus. Matthew 28:19 says, "Go therefore and make disciples of all the nations, baptizing them in the name of the Father and of the Son and of the Holy Spirit." I will agree that everyone is not called to the ministry of a pastor, evangelist, or teacher, but this is no excuse for us not to share our testimony.

When Jesus went to the well in Samaria, He had an appointment to change the life of the Samaritan woman. If you read the story all the way through, you will see a marked difference between Jesus' treatment of her and the hearts of the disciples. Jesus was killing her old life with the love and kindness of His Father. He showed her God's true compassion. His kindness allowed Him to enter in to the core of her heart and begin to clean it out. His kindness changed her life so much that she had to tell the other people in Samaria about Him. She did this at the risk of being ridiculed for her lifestyle. She showed the boldness of a veteran Christian even though she was only minutes old. The people of Samaria believed her testimony and had to go see Jesus for themselves. They probably left Him thinking, "What she said was awesome, but He made God's love sound even better in person." It was neat that their experience with Jesus was so great, but it started with the testimony of a woman that probably had a bad reputation in the town. To me, that is the awesome part of the whole story. But I must go back to the kindness of Jesus. If He spoke to her as the disciples did to Him, about her, the whole encounter would have been different. The woman would have left unchanged by the kindness and compassion of God. She would have never received the understanding that a life born from God was both complete and full of purpose.

It all starts with kindness. Why do I say that? I have to go back to a very old saying, "You never get a second chance to make a good first impression." We, as Christians, need to make the kindness of God the first thing that anyone sees. People need to see that we are Christians by our actions without having to ask if we are a Christian. Verbal testimony is powerful, but visual testimony is probably the first thing that people will encounter from us.

We have been given an incredible weapon of warfare in kindness. Kindness destroys the power of the enemy because it undermines his foundations of hatred, anger, envy, selfish ambitions, etc. There isn't much that can stand in the way of kindness. Yes, it can be very difficult to display kindness when the enemy sends a barrage of artillery at us. When he thinks that he has us on the ropes and we can still throw a smile at the enemy, he has to fall back and regroup. God will sustain you in those difficult times. He said in James 4:7, "Therefore submit to God. Resist the devil and he will flee from you." God is prepared to fight for us if we submit. We have to get over the idea that we can simply resist the devil. If we do not submit to God first, the devil will eat us for lunch. We must first submit to God. We have to act like pro wrestlers do when they get in a bind. We have to get close enough to God so we can submit to His strength and let Him take over the fight. Let God fight our battles when we show kindness to others.

I can tell you firsthand that living a life of kindness is a lot easier to live than fear, anger, and selfishness. Kindness has allowed me to meet so many incredible people. Kindness has allowed my marriage to grow to new heights. Kindness will make you look more like God than you have ever been. So, as I conclude, I plead with you to "kill them with kindness."

GOODNESS

In recent chapters I have been discussing the weapons of our warfare that are contained in Galatians 5:21, 22—the fruit of the Spirit. As I have read this passage over the years, I have often stumbled over the apparent repetition that it contains. I have been confused about kindness and goodness being two separate items, until recently. While in prayer about this chapter, I sought the Lord for revelation about the simple word goodness.

We have all heard the phrase "God is good," and I would think that most of us struggle with minimizing God to just being good. I still have a hard time saying that He is good when I feel in my heart that He is the epitome of all that is excellent and perfect. How can God just be good? Jesus said in Matthew 19:17, "Why do you call me good? No one is good but One, that is, God." Even Jesus used the term good to describe God, and we know that Jesus never minced His words. He always meant exactly what he said. I believe that if we take a deeper look at goodness, we might appreciate how good God really is.

Goodness, by definition, can mean several things, and as I list them you will probably begin to get the true understanding. Here we go: the state of being good; moral excellence; virtue; excellence of quality; the best part of anything; integrity; honesty; uprightness.

Wow, I think that these describe God in a very real and personal way. Now I know that these alone do not complete a true picture of God, but they give us a pretty good start. How does this apply to us as His children though? I believe that goodness is part of the foundation that forms us into the image of God.

If goodness is "the state of being good," then I would say that it must be in the very core of who we are. It must override everything that tries to make us do the wrong things. Without goodness being at the forefront of all that we do, we will not display kindness, gentleness, patience, love, joy, longsuffering, and self-control. I am not trying to say that goodness is greater than the other fruits of the Spirit, but I don't see us fulfilling God's Word without it being deep within us.

We display kindness toward others because of goodness. You might be mentally picturing all of the kind people you know and believe that they are good people. They may be, but goodness is not a part-time job. Goodness, if it is as deep as we need it to be, is a 24/7 activity. Those that are lost but still display acts of goodness will most often be doing them publicly. We don't know what they do behind closed doors. I am not trying to judge anyone, but let me make this point: we are not justified by our works, but by our faith in Jesus Christ (Galatians 2:16). We display goodness because of our faith in Jesus, not to gain favor.

Goodness will push us to moral excellence. Proverbs 22:1 states, "A good name is rather to be chosen than great riches." It used to be that men could make a deal with only a handshake. A man was counted on by his word. A man who wanted to be found trustworthy when he said something was the shame of the town if he was found to be a liar. Moral excellence would carry you a long way, and moral corruption would get you run out of town on a rail. Moral excellence is rooted with a deep seed of goodness.

When the woman with the issue of blood touched the hem of Jesus' garment, virtue had gone out of Him. It was a tangible pouring of Himself into her, and she was made whole. I know that she was healed by the power of the Holy Spirit, and her abundant faith triggered the flow of anointing. I also believe that Jesus ministered so much out of the abundance of heaven that He radiated the goodness of God that powerfully. There were a lot of people touching Him and if He was that radiant with God, why weren't they touched by His presence? It's very simple, she wanted to be set free. The rest of them were only going after the star effect. In other words, they wanted to be able to tell others that they got close enough to touch the one who claimed to be God's messenger. She went away from there knowing that God touched her. That is a huge difference. We really do the same thing when we go to church. Many people proclaim on Monday, "I went to church yesterday." While some proclaim that, "God moved in a powerful way yesterday and I felt His presence." Sadly, they were probably talking about the same church service. We need the virtue of God to pour out from heaven everywhere we are and not just at church.

Proverbs 31 discusses the virtuous woman. I believe that the underlying message within that passage is complete selflessness. Isn't God also selfless with His love toward us? If we let God's goodness emanate from us, as His ushers, shouldn't we become more selfless as well? This will make us look more like Him because we will develop more of a servant's heart.

Psalm 7:10 says, "My defense is of God, who saves the upright in heart." If our hearts are pure in motive and deed, God is our defense. I have often used John 8:32 to calm people down after being falsely accused. I mean that their motives were questioned by others. The scripture reads, "You shall know the truth and the truth shall make you free." If you walk with an upright heart you will have a purity that is highly regarded. If questioned about your motives, which God sees from the beginning, and you are upright, God is your defense. Regardless of what others will do or say. When Joseph was tempted by Potiphar's wife, he remained upright in heart. Although he still went to prison, God was his only defense. Joseph remained upright in heart while in prison and eventually became the second in command of all Egypt. It is necessary that we also remain upright in heart even when things don't look so good, because we need God as our defender. When we react to things from a selfish heart, we will have a harder time getting through tough times. Why? Because we have placed ourselves as our own defense attorney—that is a job we cannot fulfill. We will lose the case every time if we try to do it ourselves.

To me, goodness is not just a simple explanation of God and who we should be. I know that God is love, but He demonstrates that love out of the goodness of who He is. For us, it has to resonate from every fiber of our being. If we want to reflect His image to a lost and dying world, we need to let God's goodness dictate our every action, thought, and deed. We do not need to rely on goodness as a way to check off a list of good things that we do. We need to have our faith grown strong enough that regardless of the circumstances we will choose to do good. We need to do good whether we receive any immediate payback or not. Let's take another look at Joseph. After he interpreted the dreams of the chief butler and the chief baker, he had asked the chief butler to remember him. Joseph spent some more time in prison because the chief butler forgot about him. It wasn't until Pharaoh had his own dreams that the butler remembered Joseph. When Joseph was summoned before Pharaoh, he was used by God to interpret the dreams. We do not read anywhere about Joseph being angry at the chief butler. Joseph held his peace, allowed the goodness of God to rule in his heart, and a nation was saved. Joseph knew that, just like the accusation of Potiphar's wife, this was not his fight. He knew that God was the one to receive all of the glory, honor, and praise. He knew that God is the true and righteous judge.

Do we believe that God will judge righteously over us? Do we believe that God is the lifter of our heads? Do we believe that God knows what our rewards should be? Let's forget about our rewards, let Him worry about when and how to provide the payback, and work for Him as if working for Him is reward enough. Let's allow the goodness of God to flow through us so we become like the fragrance of God. We can't be ready to give an account for what God has done if people don't see His goodness flowing. Let's be a vessel full of the good wine!

MEEKNESS

We have all heard the scripture of the Beatitudes, "The meek shall inherit the earth." It was actually first mentioned in Psalms 37:11. In today's society that almost seems unimaginable, but we must remember that God isn't finished yet. Jesus gave us plenty of warnings that tribulation would come and that Christians would be persecuted for their faith. In these times of persecution we are called to count it as a joy in our lives. It is frustrating to watch as those that don't want anything to do with God seem to be blessed beyond measure while believers seem to be scraping by. I am reminded that Jesus said in Matthew 16:26, "For what profit is it to a man if he gains the whole world and loses his own soul? Or what will a man give in exchange for his soul?" This is played out in the parable of Lazarus and the rich man—Luke 16.

The rich man seemed to have everything that he wanted in a physical sense. Lazarus, on the other hand, had nothing of his own. He was festered with sores, and dogs would come to lick his wounds. They may have been his only friends. The rich man had to know Lazarus, but only as a lowly beggar without any value. I am sure that the rich man found Lazarus to be a serious nuisance as well. When Lazarus died he was carried into Abraham's bosom where he would not be begging any more. The rich man died and was placed into hell. The apparent status change did not register with the rich man because he had asked Abraham to send Lazarus over to give him something to drink. For the first time in his life, he was full of want and could not be satisfied. What would have happened to the rich man if he had shared his wealth and made provision for his soul?

This parable does not condemn the gathering of wealth. It does, however, want us to see that we are to minister with the things that God has given to us. The more we gain wealth without first making God the center of what we do with that wealth, the more we will slowly become enslaved by the worldly systems that we are using to gain that wealth. Even if our intentions are good, if God isn't in control of our hearts, we will be working for the world.

How do the meek inherit the earth if the worldly systems seem to be in control? I know that it's hard to see the hand of God a lot of the time, but we must remain focused on Him. If you will remember the chapter on praise, I wrote about two kinds of praise offerings. One being offered to God for His majesty and the other for His provision. We have to understand that it is not about gaining stuff now, but about an inheritance that only God can give. Our heavenly, incorruptible inheritance is given great value by the Lord. In contrast, Satan offers an inheritance that places value on things that are corruptible. The main difference between the two is the fact that God has placed an incredible value on us and was willing to pay the price for our sin debt to make us joint heirs with Christ. Satan, on the other hand, tries to get us to trade and base our value on the things of this world.

When Satan tempted Jesus in the wilderness, he offered Jesus complete rule over the earthly kingdoms. There was a high price that came with that offer. Jesus would have had to bow down to Satan. That meant that Satan would really be the one in charge of it all. We are offered the same things. Satan will dangle certain temptations out in front of us, trying to get us to bite into his lure of complete surrender. We don't have to give into these temptations. We can be just like Jesus when He used the Word of God (submitted to God), turned away from the temptation (resisted the devil), and Satan had to leave Him alone (and he will flee).

It was through the Holy Spirit's power of meekness that Jesus overcame the attacks of the enemy. When Jesus was standing before Pilate, accused by the high priest, it was meekness that allowed Him to stand there without saying a word in His own defense. Jesus knew the truth of who He was and their accusations meant nothing to Him. It was meekness that allowed both Jesus and Stephen to ask God to forgive those that were killing them. It was meekness that allowed the apostles the strength to die as martyrs in the face of their enemies.

The world sees meekness as a weakness. With the dog-eat-dog, winner-take-all attitude, it's hard not to want to get your share of things. We won't seem to fit in if we appear to refrain from going after the prize. It is hard for the world to understand that the prize we are going for is far greater than anything outside of heaven. With that in mind, the church seems to get lost in its purpose because we tend to seek self-fulfillment instead of the face of God. We build these elaborate monuments for sanctuaries and think we've made the big time. We spend a lot of money building up our programs instead of seeking the face of God to see where He wants the money to go. And what does the church have to show for our efforts? 1) A divorce rate that parallels the world's divorce rate. 2) A body that doesn't know the Word of God—a lack of true discipleship. 3) A people that are mixed up in things that the Word tells us is not good for us—Harry Potter books and movies, and the Twilight, vampire movies; just to name a couple of things. The church has to separate itself from the love of this world. The world is getting confused by the mixed signals we are sending. For that matter, the people inside the church are confused because the elevated leaders of the church are not guiding with a pure light of the gospel. It's time for the church to get real. We need to get back on our foundation, which is the Word of God, and work to build the kingdom of God first. If we build His kingdom rather than our domain, we can effectively raise up a mighty, spirit-filled body of believers that can reach the lost. Instead of operating with the winner take all, bigger is better, attitude, we as a church should be living a life of meekness. Having monumental churches does not give us points on a score card. When we get more interested at changing lives with our meekness instead of changing our buildings, the body of Christ will begin to see communities turned to Christ.

Meekness plays an important role in our daily lives. Meekness allows us to surrender our right to getting angry when we are the accused. It's hard not to defend ourselves when we have an accusation brought against us. We tend to let our pride step in and say, "I'll handle this." That's usually when we start getting into trouble. With Jesus being our perfect example, He was able to hold His tongue when faced with impending judgment. His obedience to the Father was much more effective than a long discourse of His innocence. As we can see, the reward of Jesus' obedience is immeasurable. While taking on the ridicule, the pain, the anguish, and the weight of all of our sins, Jesus did not lift a hand to stop the crucifixion. Second Corinthians 13:4 states, "For though He was crucified in weakness, yet He lives by the power of God. For we are also weak in Him, but we shall live with Him by the power of God toward you." Second Corinthians 12:10 (KJV) says, "Therefore I take pleasure in infirmities, in reproaches, in necessities, in persecutions, in distresses for Christ's sake: for when I am weak, then am I strong." When Stephen was taken before his accusers, he did not spend his last moments defending himself. Stephen preached to the council all that God had done for the nation of Israel, and how they were missing the boat because of the hard hearts toward the gospel. Stephen was not weak as some would count weakness. He showed great strength in refraining from his own desires to fulfill the desires of God.

Is there anything in this world that we want to inherit anyway? Please understand that persecution will increase. We have to be ready because the world is becoming more intolerant to the things of God. The world is getting into a survivalist mode and the church is standing in the way of the tactics that will be necessary to fulfill its rage. I know that this seems like doom and gloom but let me reassure you in this: When Jesus was asked by the high priest if He was the Christ, the Son of the Blessed (Mark 14:61), Jesus replied, "I am: and you shall see the Son of Man sitting on the right hand of power, and coming in the clouds of heaven" (Mark 14:62). Matthew 25:31-34 gives an example of Jesus sitting on His throne as a judge of the nations. Revelation 19:11 tells us that Jesus will be sitting on a white horse for His second coming. Those examples all declare the awesome majesty of our Lord and Savior, the King of Kings and Lord of Lords, but let me share one more scripture that declares the heart that Jesus has for His saints. Acts 7:55, "But he (Stephen), being full of the Holy Ghost, looked up steadfastly into heaven, and saw the glory of God, and Jesus standing on the right hand of God." Wow, wow, wow! Jesus was standing up to show honor to His servant Stephen. Jesus sits on His thrown in majesty and stands up to honor His saints who take it on the chin for the glory of God. I can imagine Jesus getting really excited and saying, "Look Father, my servant Stephen is being obedient to the very end." Would God reply in this way? "Yes, Son, he kind of reminds Me of You." Do we remind God of Jesus when we react to situations in our lives? Kind of a tough question to answer at times, isn't it?

TEMPERANCE

As we continue to study the weapons of warfare, we have found that the use of these weapons will transform us into the image of Jesus Christ. With that said, temperance is no less important in our transformation. It is also very important in our daily spiritual battles. It is one of the first things that we must do in order to maintain or use any of the other weapons of our warfare. We must have temperance, self control.

As the Lord began to deal with me on this chapter, He clearly said to me, "Control self." I had never thought about reversing the two words before, but it makes complete sense. If we want to have self-control in our lives we must control our "self" nature. Temperance is not a once-in-a-while weapon. We have to use self-control in every facet of our lives. Our old sin nature is looking for any crack that it can find to get back into our lives. It never rests from looking for opportunities. Our spirit man must be put in charge.

In 2 Peter 1:5-10, Peter is very adamant about Christians living a godly life. We do this by adding to our faith, virtue, and to our virtue, (biblical) knowledge; to our knowledge, temperance; to temperance we add patience; to patience, godliness; to godliness, brotherly kindness and with brotherly kindness we add brotherly love. Peter went on to say that if we are lacking in these things, we are blind and have forgotten that we have been purged from our old sins. He said that we must be diligent in these things concerning our Christian walk, to be sure of our calling. He then said that if we do these things we will not fall. In other words, if we make a choice of making this our life style and do not waver from them, we won't fall. They are all distinct traits that we have to build upon as Christians because they build us into the image of God by Christ Jesus.

Brothers and sisters, don't be fooled to think that one day of living this out is a committed way toward a life of godly living. We have to decide that this is how we are going to live all of the time. Is it going to be hard? Yes. Is it possible for us to live this out? Yes. Jesus, as our perfect example, would never have called us to do anything or live a certain way if we could not bring it to pass. If He showed us a way that was impossible for us to complete, He would have been a liar and a failure. There is nothing that He hasn't called you to be that you can't be. If He knew that Peter could not walk on water, Jesus would not have called him out of the boat. Too many times, His calling and our expectations don't match up. We fall short of His calling all of the time and it's not because of Him. It is a weakness in our own flesh that keeps us from fulfilling our calling and destiny.

We must bring our flesh into complete subjection of His Spirit. James 4:7 says, "Therefore submit to God. *Resist the devil* and he will flee from you" *(emphasis mine)*. We cannot resist the devil without first submitting to God. I am sure that you can think of a thousand ways to submit to God before resisting the devil, but self-control is the key. Why? The enemy will attack you in ways that will cause you to submit your flesh to him. Whether it is food, drugs, fornication, etc., the enemy wants us to submit our flesh to him. Let's take a look at the way he tempted Jesus in the wilderness. When Jesus had been fasting for forty days, Satan tempted His flesh with something to eat. He wanted Jesus to submit to His hunger rather than what God had called Him to do. Satan then took Jesus to the pinnacle of the temple to get Him to submit His flesh to his version of the Word of God. And lastly, Satan told Jesus that He could be ruler of all of the kingdoms of earth. This would be submitting His flesh in worship of Satan. In all three temptations, Jesus exhibited a great amount of self-control and fulfilled the Word of God and His calling.

In our human form, it is very difficult to fast one meal. After a few hours our stomachs will begin to rumble and every scent of food seems to drift under our nose. It almost doesn't seem fair. We begin to think, "Doesn't everyone know that I am fasting?" If we fast for the right reasons and put God in the center, we will find it easier to fulfill the things of the spirit of God rather than our flesh. But any time we do things that appear to be godly with the desire to be the center of attention, we will fall short of the Word of God and our calling.

We have to realize that our desires must submit to the will of God. If we want any victory in our lives, God's will must become our own. It is His desire for us to live in complete victory, regardless of the tests that come our way. Remember this, God is not our tempter. He is not surprised at all by the tests and trials that come our way, but He always provides a way to complete those tests with victory rather than defeat.

The more that we can operate in self-control, the more we will look like the image of Jesus Christ. Let's take a look at the very walk of Jesus. Throughout the gospels, we see Jesus operating in full control of every situation. However, when He went into the temple, it appears that He completely lost control of Himself. It did seem a bit out of character for Jesus to explode like that, but allow me to make two points. Number 1: Jesus was resetting the need for reverence in the house of God; something that we severely lack today. Number 2: He was in complete control of His faculties at the time, but when He handled all of the other situations, under the appearance of complete control, the war in the heavenly realm had the appearance of the rage in the temple. Well, how does that apply to us today? We have the same authority as Jesus does when dealing with the enemy of our souls. When we utilize the weapons of warfare, and namely self-control, it is the same heavenly warfare raging around us.

When Jesus departed the ship as He arrived in the country of the Gadarenes; He was immediately approached by the man with an unclean spirit. The unclean spirit recognized the authority of Jesus. Why?

Jesus carried the authority of God, but not for His own gain. Jesus carried and used God's authority to glorify His Father. Brothers and sisters, we carry that same authority. Everywhere we go, God's authority is within us. The spirit of the enemy should recognize the authority of God. If we desire to glorify God with everything that we do, the authority of God has the power to bring us victory. It's not to say that God's authority lacks any power though. God won't share His glory with anyone. So if we try to operate in the power of the Holy Spirit and our motivation is for personal gain, we will ultimately fail, and the enemy will win.

If we want to walk in complete victory in our lives, we must walk with self-control. We will be able to slay the giants that stand before us just as David killed Goliath. We will fulfill the calling that God has for us in our lives. His greatest desire is for us to be the express image of Jesus Christ on this earth. That is His first calling of every believer. Where God calls us, He will lead us. Where He leads us, He will equip us. Where He equips us, He will bring us victory. We will not go into any battle, struggle, or temptation that God won't equip us to handle. With temperance, we take on the very spirit of God.

So let us, by the spirit of God, gain control of ourselves, our flesh, and walk worthy of the call that He has for us.

FEAR

In today's society we are taught at an early age to fear things. We, then, teach our children to not touch a hot stove, to not talk to strangers, and to not run with scissors in their hands. All of these are legitimate things that can bring harm to our children. As they grow up, we start to refrain from that teaching so they can learn to grow up not being afraid of everything. When we were kids we would dare to do things that we would not think of today. We seemed to have a little daredevil inside of us that would try almost anything. The more we could do without getting hurt would prompt us to try even more dangerous stunts. In fact, a lot of times when we were young, we were not aware of the danger. We wanted to see how far we could push the envelope without any major injuries. Even if we were injured, we would often try it again to overcome that fear.

Fear of anything seems to disappear over time. In the mid-1990s, a slogan came out called "No Fear." It was very popular at the time and was seen on everything from T-shirts and hats to bumper stickers. It permeated the hearts and minds of a generation and taught them to not fear anything. I am not sure how much it actually worked, but I don't believe that the church helped the situation.

Several years after the "No Fear" slogan was running amuck, someone came out with the Christian alternative. To no surprise it said "Fear Not." The Word of God tells us not to be afraid of the things of this world. There are a lot of Christians that need to take hold of this truth in scripture. However, the Word of God is not to be used as a flippant phrase. Hebrews 4:12 says, "The word of God is living and powerful, and sharper than any two edged sword, piercing even to the division of the soul and spirit, and the joints and the marrow, and is a discerner of the thoughts and intents of the heart." If we treat God's Word like a whimsical thread of speech, we won't be able to use it with its full power because we won't respect it's authority over the kingdoms of this world.

Allow me to make a point here about "Christian Alternatives" to something from a worldly origin. The church should not be coming up with the alternatives. The church should be setting the standard that is copied by the world. Remember that Satan counterfeits what God creates. If the church had been teaching a fear of God, there would not have been a reason for someone to come up with "No Fear."

So, what have we ended up with? What have we accomplished with all of this "No Fear/Fear Not" training? I believe that we developed a generation of young believers in God who do not fear God. I am not talking about a fear in which people are afraid of God as if He was like a monster in a movie. And I'm not saying that they don't love God. I mean the reverent fear of Him because He is mighty and powerful; awesome in splendor and reigns on His throne in heaven.

We as a church really don't have a true fear of God. You may be asking, or have already asked what the topic of fear has to do with the weapons of our warfare. To be honest, I was a little taken back when God revealed it to me. But as He began to reveal Himself to me, I started to shout praises to His name. Let's see what the Lord said in His Word about fear.

> Psalm 111:10–"The fear of the Lord is the beginning of wisdom."

> Proverbs 1:7–"The fear of the Lord is the beginning of knowledge."

> Proverbs 9:10–"The fear of the Lord is the beginning of wisdom."

It must be pretty important for us to have the understanding of where wisdom and knowledge originates. When we truly fear the Lord, we can tap into the wisdom that begins at His throne. He gives us understanding of Himself when we fear Him.

When we have the understanding of who God is and revere Him, we can stand on the scriptures with the full assurance that God is our strong tower. Psalm 27:1 says, "The Lord is my light and my salvation; whom shall I fear? The Lord is the strength of my life; of whom shall I be afraid." When we fear God, we have no need to fear the world.

So, from a worldly sense, where does fear come from? Why do we have a fear of things instead of God? When we live in disobedience, we fear judgment. We fear being persecuted for our faith because we don't have the level of trust for God that we need. We fear acts of nature such as hurricanes, earthquakes, and floods. We are afraid of the unknown. And we are afraid of death. Fear can also be very crippling for some people. It can actually have such a grip on someone to make them afraid of leaving their homes. They cannot function in any normal capacity of human existence.

There is one more thing that I want to say about the wrong kind of fear. It will hinder our worship of God. If we fear everything but God, we will not (cannot) worship Him in spirit and in truth. Why? Because we will be in a place that causes us to fear what others will think about our singing, dancing, and general lack of ability to perform. It's not about performing before God. It's about letting Him have His way in our lives and bring us into a closer relationship with Him.

Why do we fear the people with whom we go to church with? Aren't we all on the same team? It is time for us to forget about the one standing to our right and left and truly worship God. He desires for us to really let go of ourselves and allow Him to wrap Himself completely around us. He wants to help us shed the weights that so easily beset us. He wants to pour out His spirit on us like He did when they dedicated the temple in 2 Chronicles 5. He wants to pour Himself over us like He did on the day of Pentecost. But what did they have that we don't have? Unity in the spirit.

Then how do we get unified in the spirit like them? Have such a reverence for God that we don't care about anything else but pleasing Him. We play our instruments with the only purpose of pleasing Him. We sing with voices that no matter how good or bad they sound in the natural, we want to please God. When we can do that, we will have true unity in the spirit.

The fear of God will deliver us from the fear of the world. Romans 8:31 says, "…if God is for us, who can be against us." This scripture does not guarantee that we won't be attacked or have hardships; however, it does guarantee that God will always be on our side. He will always be fighting for us.

Proverbs 8:13 says, "The fear of the Lord is to hate evil: pride and arrogance, and the evil way, and the perverse mouth I hate." When we fear the Lord, we follow after His heart and run from those things that will place a wall between God and us. The walls of pride, envy, hatred of others, jealousy, and malice toward the success of others; God won't stand for it. If we work in these things rather than the gifts of the spirit, we will not see what God can do through us because we are looking at others rather than looking at God. Stop looking around and start looking up. If we will begin to rejoice in the spiritual success of others, God will pour more of Himself over us.

It is true that we need to walk without fear. We do not need to be afraid of anything that pertains to the things of this world. Second Timothy 1:7 says, "God has not given us a spirit of fear, but of power and of love and of a sound mind."

If we put on the mind of Christ we will operate with love and power. We can share the love of Christ without the fear of rejection because we are not the one getting rejected. We can operate under the power and anointing of the Holy Spirit by praying over people without the fear of failure. It is not our power that we operate in. If we try to do the things of God with our own power or authority, we will quickly fail and wear out. In the book of John, Jesus operated without fear because He was directing all of the glory to God the Father. He was not operating under the power of Jesus alone. The Holy Spirit was guiding Him every step of the way and pouring the anointing of God over His work. Jesus operated with the power and love of the Holy Spirit. He did not allow fear to enter into any situation.

We have the same authority to operate in the same power and love of the Holy Spirit. Jesus said that the works that He did, we shall do. He even said that we would do greater works. I know that it's hard to comprehend, but we have to stop trying to operate the gifts of God through the filter of fear. We need to have a reverence for God that is so strong that Acts 10:38 is fulfilled everywhere we go. We need to have extreme fear. A fear that allows us to stand at the edge of a cliff with our toes hanging over the edge, and when God calls us to trust Him, we fall forward into His arms.

When we have our fear of God grown to this level, we will operate in the fullness of the power of God. We will be able to fine-tune our hearing to notice the gentle whispers of His voice. And when He speaks to us, we will feel the caress of His love come over us.

Brothers and sisters, we are called to enjoy the deeper things of the Lord. We are called to rejoice over His majesty. We are called to be passionately in love with our Father. Would you like to know why we are called to do those things for Him—because He enjoys digging into the deepest parts of us and recreating us into the image of His Son. When He sees His Son inside of us, He rejoices over the majesty that is birthed inside. And the Father is passionately in love with us.

Our fear of God will allow us to rest in His strong tower. Our fear of God is the shadow of His wings where we can hide. The enemy of our soul hates it when we fear God because his attempts at creating havoc in our lives are destroyed by the power of God. It's not that we are operating in the power of God, but it's the power of God operating in us.

Fear God and be free of judgment. Fear God and be free of ridicule. Fear God and be free of a broken heart. Fear God and be free of pride. Fear God and be free!

CONFESSION

We learned in an earlier chapter that forgiveness is a powerful weapon of our warfare. It offers a release from the weight of sin that we cannot possibly bear. I am not just talking about being forgiven either. It also applies to when we forgive the wrongs of others against us. The enemy of our soul does not want us to walk in forgiveness, no matter which side we are on. There is, however, one more weight that the enemy does not want us to know about. He does not want us to know how powerful confession is to us. I am not talking about getting into a confession booth and talking it out with a priest either. I believe that there may be some merit to how the Catholics bring the confessions of their sins, because it allows people to get the acts of sin off their chest.

That is what I want to talk about with this weapon of warfare. Confession is the unloading of sin as if it were a bag of rotten fruit. That is exactly what sin is, rotten fruit. It is fruit of the old man that we used to live like.

Sir Isaac Newton, the man who had the revelation about gravity, realized three other laws of motion. These laws relate to how objects move and how resistance changes how objects move. All of this is relative to the force and mass of the objects. A heavy object takes a lot of force to be moved while lighter objects need less. These laws are summarized with this statement: Every action has an equal and opposite reaction. In other words, if you have to push your car, the mass of the car will offer resistance to being pushed. In order to be moved, the mass of an object has to be overcome by the force trying to push it. I know that Mr. Newton was relating this to physical objects, but I see that it also has some powerful spiritual connotations.

If we do not go to God with our weaknesses, it will be as if we load up the weight of sin. Hebrews 12:1 (KJV) says, "Wherefore seeing we also are compassed about with so great a cloud of witnesses, let us lay aside every weight, and the sin which so easily ensnares us, and let us run with patience the race that is set before us." This verse speaks to us about laying down the weights that hold us down. These weights, if gone unchecked, become a mass that makes it hard for us to move forward for the Lord. It keeps us from being the kingdom people that God created us to be. It also says that these sins easily ensnare us. We have a great cloud of witnesses set before us—both heavenly, and those who God has placed in our path. There are people available in our lives we can discuss our weaknesses with. We need to start opening up to the Lord, and those who we believe that we can confide in, to shed the weight of sin.

When we become grappled with the guilt of sin, we tend to hide them because we are too embarrassed to confess. This is exactly what the enemy wants. The more he can convince us to keep quiet about our weaknesses, the heavier the burden becomes. It seems like it takes more force to even move around. He will make us feel so guilty that we won't even want to go to church, out of fear that someone will see the sin stamped right on our foreheads. Yet church is the one place for us to be set free. If the body of Christ does its job, it will surround the wounded sheep and help it heal. Unfortunately, the church usually acts as judge and jury with the soul that is wounded. Instead of acting like Christ when He was confronted with the woman caught in adultery, we are the ones ready to throw stones. We can't condone the sin, but we can love the one caught in the trap of sin. In 1 Peter 4:8 it says, "And above all things have fervent love for one another, for love will cover a multitude of sins."

Micah 6:8, "He has shown you, O man, what is good; And what does the Lord require of you but to do justly, to love mercy, and to walk humbly with your God?"

Our sins separate us from God. The only way we can get things right with God is to confess our sins to Him. His unlimited grace will always allow us to come to Him. Yet we get so blinded by the lies of the enemy. Satan will always tell us, "You have really messed up this time; there is no way that you can be forgiven for that. You need to hide from God on this one because you just asked Him to forgive you for that two weeks ago. He forgave you then, but here you are, already committing the same sin." Does any of this sound familiar? All Satan wants to do is to raise a little seed of doubt about how faithful and gracious God really is. If he can convince us with this deception, he will keep us from going to God with our problems.

Our sin can separate us from others. If we do something that offends or hurts others, Satan will do one of several things to drive a wedge between us. 1. He will want us to hide what we have done by convincing us that the person may never find out. 2. He will cause us to allow pride to convince us that it wasn't really that bad or deny that we even did what it was we were accused of. 3. He will cause us to get angry and act as if it was the other person's fault. All of these things are not of God. All Satan needs is a moment of our time to get us listening to his voice instead of the voice of God.

It is God that desires reconciliation between us and Him, and between us and others. We are going to sin against God and others. This is a fact. But what we do after we sin is up to us. Do we allow our spirit man to confess and seek forgiveness, or do we allow our old sin nature to have his way? Reconciliation cannot take place without confession. We can't be released from our burdens if we do not seek help from the Lord.

The weight of sin is like a yoke used on a pair of oxen to pull a heavy load. Yet, with us, Satan yokes us with the shame of sin and we are the only one carrying the load. It is a burden that we carry because we don't know how to be released. We don't have the confidence in the grace of God that He will break the yoke from off our necks.

Leviticus 26:13–"I am the Lord your God, who brought you forth out of the land of Egypt, that you should not be their slaves; and I have broken the bands of your yoke, and made you go upright."

God desires for us to be free from the weight of sin.

Isaiah 9:4–"For You have broken the yoke of his burden and the staff of his shoulder, the rod of his oppressor, as in the day of Midian."

Isaiah 10:27–"And it shall come to pass in that day, that his burden shall be taken away from off thy shoulder, and his yoke from off your neck, and the yoke shall be destroyed because of the anointing oil."

Isaiah 58:6–"Is not this the fast that I have chosen? To loose the bonds of wickedness, to undo the heavy burdens, and to let the oppressed go free, and that you break every yoke?"

Jesus said in Matthew 11:29, 30—"Take My yoke upon you and learn from me, for I am gentle and lowly in heart, and you will find rest for your souls. For my yoke is easy and my burden is light."

Galatians 5:1- "Stand fast therefore in the liberty by which Christ has made us free, and do not be entangled again with a yoke of bondage."

God does not place the burden of guilt upon us. The Holy Spirit will convict us in our hearts, but not for the purpose of pushing us away from the Lord. We are convicted by Him to draw near to God and be renewed in spirit. God desires us to portray the image of Christ, but when we are riddled with the burden of sin, we look nothing like Him. When we go to the Lord for the Holy Spirit to cleanse our hearts, we again shine with the righteousness of Jesus.

Confession empties our basket of sin. When the enemy accuses us of a transgression before God, we can't let pride stand between us and the throne. We need to act as if we are standing on a mountaintop and shout from the top of our lungs; It's true, I did it, and I am sorry. God, will you forgive me? If we will quickly confess our weakness to the Lord, He will quickly forgive us. If we are forgiven, we won't be carrying the burden of sin on our shoulders.

Now, we do have to stay away from those things that easily entrap us. It is much easier to abstain from a sin if we are not in a place to entertain it. We need to know what tempts us and run away from it whenever it is around.

Confession and forgiveness go hand in hand. When we don't activate either of these in our lives, we will be miserable. Without confession or forgiveness we bind up the grace of God. We thrust upon us, and others, a yoke that can only be broken with the love of God.

Open up to God. He is waiting and wanting to pour His grace over you like a refreshing waterfall. We will come out clean and refreshed.

THANKFULNESS

I recently read this statement on www.inspirationline.com: "It's not what we say about our blessings, but how we use them is the true measure of our thankfulness." Think about that for a minute. It is important to say "Thank you," but when we show our gratitude in some form or fashion, there seems to be a lot more meaning to the words. There is a real and deeper mystery to being thankful that most of us don't understand. James 2:20 says, "Faith without works is dead." The chapter concludes with this thought in verse 26: "For as the body without the spirit is dead, so faith without works is dead also." I know that this is a sobering thought. It is supposed to be.

How can I compare thankfulness and works? Well, let's look at a few scenarios from the Word of God. In Luke 17, Jesus entered into a village where ten lepers had met Him from a distance. They cried out for mercy from the King of Mercy. At the command of Jesus, they showed themselves to the priest and they were cleansed. After they saw that they were made clean, verses 15 and 16 state, "And one of them, when he saw that he was healed, returned, and with a loud voice glorified God, and fell down on his face at His feet, giving Him thanks. Jesus asked him, 'Were there not ten cleansed? But where are the other nine?'" Jesus didn't doubt that the other nine had been healed of their leprosy. I am also quite certain that they were all very thankful to God for their healing. However, one man did not just verbally express his gratitude for his healing. He showed his appreciation by going back to Jesus and worshiped at His feet. The difference between this man and the other nine is this fact: he will be less likely to forget where his healing came from. He will be the one that testifies of the goodness of God. He will tell everyone that God showed him mercy when he did not deserve mercy. This man will use his blessing to glorify God.

Again in Luke we have another incredible story of a person displaying their gratitude to Jesus. In chapter 7, beginning with verse 36, Jesus had been invited to eat at Simon's house. Simon was a Pharisee whose motives were probably less than honorable. He probably did not invite Jesus to dinner in the hopes that Jesus would expound on the mercy of God and be convinced of the deity of Jesus. The underlying plan of the Pharisees was to find a way to successfully challenge the wisdom of Jesus.

As the guests of Simon were eating, a woman of the city came up to Jesus with tears in her eyes. This woman began to wash the feet of Jesus with her tears and dry them with her hair. She also anointed His feet and head with expensive oil. Simon and the other Pharisees were very upset that this woman was even in Simon's house and questioned the authenticity of Jesus as a prophet. Jesus, knowing Simon's disgust of the woman, began to tell him that she was more honorable than him because she had washed Jesus' feet and he did not. He said that Simon should have greeted Him with a kiss when she had continually kissed His feet since she arrived. He continued to explain that she had anointed his head with oil and Simon did not.

Jesus had explained why the woman was so grateful in the story of two men who had owed a lot of money. One owed 500 pence and the other owed 50 pence; both men had been forgiven of their debt. Jesus asked Simon which one of them would love the creditor more? Simon correctly answered, "I suppose the one who was forgiven most." He said that she had been forgiven much so she loved Him much. The woman knew that her life was a real mess, and God had set her free. She openly showed her gratitude to God in a way that she could not tell others about His goodness and mercy.

When Jesus finished His parable, He basically told Simon and the other Pharisees that this woman loved God more than they did. Her gratitude was expressed by her works of love. Her display of affection was not born out of a "look at me" attitude. Her affection was born from her new birth in God by Jesus Christ. She only wanted God on display because He loosed the chains in her life that had so easily had her bound.

Let's now go into Samaria. There we find a woman at the well of her ancestors. She probably thought that this day would be like any other day. However, when Jesus entered into her life, she would never be the same.

This woman had been married to five men and was currently living with a man who was not her husband. She was taken by surprise when Jesus asked her to give Him a drink of water. The moments that followed changed this woman forever. Jesus told her about her life, allowing her to see its uncleanness. But instead of pouring on shame and ridicule, Jesus began to share with her that God wanted to give her living water. With this water she would never thirst again. She would never thirst again for the things that left her empty and void of love and satisfaction. Her soul would be filled up, as her spirit would be set free.

Upon feeling this release in her life, the Samaritan woman did not just say thank you and continue on with her life. She became a woman on a mission to share the news about this living water and how refreshing it is. I am sure that this woman had a bad reputation in Samaria, but she did not let that keep her from telling of the glory of God. She went back to her hometown to tell everyone about Jesus. John 4:39 says that the Samaritans believed in Jesus because of her testimony. Her testimony was the work of her gratitude and because of her love and thankfulness many came to know Christ and entered into the joy of the Lord.

How do these three stories from the Word apply to our lives today? Spiritually speaking, there are a lot of opportunities to show our thankfulness toward the Lord. Most of us can fit into the category of the Samaritan woman to show our gratitude. We can offer up a testimony for what God has done for us. Whenever we testify of God's goodness or mercy or

His undying love for us, the enemy of our soul gets angry. He does not want God to receive any glory for anything. So, if he can keep us from giving a testimony of thanks, or taking it a step further by telling someone about God's grace through Jesus, he hinders us from advancing the kingdom of God. True thankfulness for the Lord brings Him glory and advances His kingdom. It draws others into His grace.

As my pastor has said many times, when we receive a healing it's not only for our benefit. We should lay hands on someone else, pray the prayer of faith, and see the work of the Lord setting them free. If we have the bonds of an illness released off of ourselves, our thankfulness for the release should compel us to see someone else set free.

There is one main difference in these three people, and I hope that you were able to see it. Nonetheless, I will share it anyway. The first two came back to worship the Lord, out of gratitude. They wanted to go the extra mile with their thanksgiving. What they did stands as memorial in the Word of God. We should, at the very least, worship the Lord for setting us free. However, the woman at the well used her gift of thanksgiving to advance the kingdom of God. Now I'm not saying that she is any more important than the other two. But, like her, we are able to tell others what God has done for us. We have been blessed to be a blessing. We have been changed to be used of God, to change others.

Psalm 34:8 says, "O taste and see that the Lord is good." There are not a lot of people who have tasted nor have they seen that the Lord is good. We have been given the living water of God. God wants to pour that living water through us, His vessels. One way that we can be a vessel fit for use is to live a life of thankfulness.

When we operate with a thankful heart in our lives, it produces joy. Then, joy produces strength in God. A thankful/joyful heart provides an opportunity to share the love of God through Jesus. It is so easy for us to be thankful in the good times, but when things are difficult, we find it hard to give thanks. James 1:2 says, "My brethren, count it all joy when you fall into various trials." As stated above, we need to be a vessel of thankfulness. If we cannot display a thankful heart for God, people can't taste and see that He is good.

If your joy and thankfulness is the same at all times, the light of Jesus shines forth and He changes the atmosphere. Your life is a reflection of Him and, like moths to a flame, people are drawn in and consumed by His presence. Living a thankful life brings glory to the Lord. Why? Because being thankful causes us to direct our love and gratitude toward God rather than ourselves. God desires to work with humility. He is the One who provides kingdom promotion, and it is our duty to be thankful for where He places us in the work of the kingdom. Yet there are too many of us who are ambitious and impatient. Ambition and impatience leads to an ungrateful heart that is not eager to please the Father.

Let us put on an attitude of gratitude. Let us begin today and everyday with having a thankful heart. I understand that life gets tough sometimes but God will order the steps of the righteous. Even when things don't look promising, let's be thankful that God is in charge of it all. Let us remember that He still sits on the throne and Jesus is seated at His right hand. His love for us is unending and His mercy outweighs His judgment. That by itself is a lot to be thankful for.

UNITY

Until now, every weapon of warfare has been written with the individual person in mind. Each previous chapter has provided some insight for us to fight our everyday battles on the personal level. While our spiritual walk is personal, we have to remember that we are all a part of the body of Christ. With that said, the only way we can have complete victory as a part of the body of Christ is to have complete unity with the body of Christ. What do I mean by saying we must have complete unity with the body of Christ?

Let me preface my answer by saying this, we will not always be in agreement with other parts of the body. First and foremost, our complete unity begins with complete surrender to God. You may be asking how this will bring unity in the body. When we surrender to God, we must have, as the center of our focus, His plan of salvation. We must get into agreement that Jesus Christ died on the cross for our sins, was buried, and rose again on the third day. We must agree that all of this happened for the redemption of our sins. When we can agree on this, we can get beyond the other things that bring division.

Why is unity so important? Let's take a look in Mark 3. In this chapter, Jesus had anointed the disciples to be with Him, to be sent to preach, to have power to heal sickness, and to cast out demons. When the multitude came together, the scribes said that Jesus had Beelzebub and cast out demons by the prince of devils. Jesus' explanation about unity is amazing in this passage because He even said that Satan needed to be unified in his efforts. He said, beginning in verse 23:

> How can Satan cast out Satan? If a kingdom is divided against itself, that kingdom cannot stand. And if a house is divided against itself, that house cannot stand. And if Satan has risen up against himself, and is divided, he cannot stand, but has an end.

In everything there has to be unity if there is going to be any measureable success. I must note here that no matter how unified Satan is against an individual or the church, his end will come. He has already lost the war.

Satan has done a pretty good job at causing division in the body of Christ. I don't mean to give him any credit, but we have to look at the facts. Satan does not mind if we worship God, and he does not mind if we go to church. With that said, he also desires to cause us to support different doctrines of our faith. For example, part of the body believes in healing miracles and other parts do not. Some believe in the baptism of the Holy Spirit while others do not. Some people believe in the gifts of the Spirit while others don't believe that God has provided any gifts to His church. He wants to create divisions with how we worship. He wants to create divisions in every aspect of the function of the body of Christ. We get so divided by the things we don't agree upon, we lose the fact that we are on the same team. We end up saying, I am Baptist and I have no need of those who are charismatic. Or, I am Pentecostal so I have no need of the Catholics. All this division and we fail to read 1 Corinthians 12. It is here that the Apostle Paul instructs us that although body of Christ has many members, it is still one body. There is not any part of the body that can say, "I have no need of you." We must focus on the truth of God's Word and unity as never before. Again, we won't always be in agreement, but we can still be unified. For example, a married couple can have differences of opinions and still be unified by their love for each other. In spite of our differences, we must remain unified by the love of Jesus. Remember, Jesus said in John 13:34-35, "A new commandment I give to you, that you love one another; as I have loved you, that you also love one another. By this all will know that you are my disciples, if you have love for one another."

So I ask this question, what are the results of a lack of unity in the church? The lack of unity results in a lack of power and authority in worship, evangelism, and discipleship. How can I be so sure of this? Let's look in Ephesians 4. Starting with verse 11, the apostle Paul says that God gave apostles, prophets, evangelists, pastors, and teachers for a specific purpose. The purpose of the five-fold ministry offices is to equip the saints for the working of ministry and for the edifying of the body of Christ. Let me rephrase that statement. God did not give us the apostles, prophets, evangelists, pastors, and teachers so they could equip each other for ministry and edify themselves. He gave them so they could equip the body of Christ for ministry. Let me continue with this. In verse 15 and 16 Paul wrote,

> Speaking the truth in love, may grow up in all things into Him who is the head—Christ—from whom the whole body, joined and knit together by what every joint supplies, according to the effective working by which every part does its share, causes growth of the body for the edifying of itself in love.

> In other words, every part has a purpose in ministry and has to do its part so that the body grows, becomes stronger, and is edified in love.

When we fulfill our calling within the body of Christ, the body grows and is strengthened. Yet, this is only one part of the truth in God's Word. There is another purpose for us as a part of the body of Christ. You see, this still has to do with fulfilling the burden of the Father to see people give their hearts to Him. For this we have to go to John 17:6-20. Jesus has prayed for God to keep His disciples and to sanctify them by His truth. Beginning in verse 20 Jesus began to pray for everyone who would believe in Him because of the word and testimony of the disciples. He said,

> I do not pray for these alone, meaning the disciples, but also for those who will believe in me

through their word; that they all may be one, as you, Father, are in me and I in you; that they also may be one in us, that the world may believe that you sent me.

This is a powerful prayer for our unity, and it is filled with yet another reason why we need to be unified in our faith. Jesus asked the Father that we would be one as they are one with each other and that we would be one with them. The reason such unity is important is so the world will know that Jesus was sent by His Father. If the world sees unity in the faith, it sees Jesus sent by the Father. If the world sees confusion and discord it cannot see that Jesus was sent by the Father. When we do not walk in unity we will send mixed signals to the world and they won't know which signal is correct.

We have to come to the realization that our unity, or lack of it, has souls hanging in the balance. We have lost people coming into our churches every Sunday looking for truth, and they end up leaving because they don't see truth. For example, when a lost person sees that more than half of the congregation will not worship the God who saved them, why would they need to give their heart to Him? When the world sees that the divorce rate in the church is as high as theirs, how can the church say that marriage is supposed to be between one man and one woman? When the world sees what appears to be money grubbing by television evangelists, they don't see anything different than what the government or corporate America does. All the world sees is the business of the church rather than humility of the church.

We have all heard it said that there is strength in numbers. That is true, but, with God, our strength is in obedience. God can do a lot with a few people who will get unified in their purpose for the kingdom of God. Jesus started everything with twelve men who gave up their lives to follow after Him. The apostles turned the world upside down with their commitment to serving the Lord and spreading the gospel of Christ. Beloved brothers and sisters in Christ, we have to get down to the business of sharing the cross of Christ without any thought for accolades and reward. The apostles, save John, who was exiled on the Isle of Patmos, were martyred for their faith. What are we willing to do to become a unified body for Christ? Are we willing to go where He says go? Are we willing to do what He says do? Are we willing to lay down our lives for the sake of the gospel? That in itself can mean several things though. We can give up our lives as we know it by getting rid of our worldly possessions, or we can literally lay our lives down in death or both. Regardless of which, unity in the body comes at a price. Are we willing to pay? Are we willing to lay down our denominational/doctrinal differences to make sure that every soul possible has a place in heaven? I, for one, am not sure that this will happen, but I do know that Jesus will return for a spotless bride. I surely don't want to be counted as a spot.

CONCLUSION

Throughout this book we have been on a journey to discover the different weapons that God has given to us for our victory. Although this book is at its end, it is my prayer is that God gives each of you a deeper revelation of Himself and reveals even more ways that lead you to complete victory over the enemy of your soul. We must continually seek ways to grow in the Lord, and as we do, God will give us revelation about Himself. And as we gain understanding in Him we must use that understanding to overcome the wicked one. We must also help others overcome the enemy so the body of Christ will be presented as a spotless bride to Christ.

We have to understand that there is warfare going on every day. What we see in the news is called carnal warfare, which includes military warfare. Spiritual warfare encompasses so much more than we can see because it involves things that influences people without their knowledge. Although there are vast differences within both types of warfare, there are similarities too. Just like a military fights for its own nation, the church fights for God. There is one huge difference. While both a regular army and God's army are issued weapons that tear down the enemy strongholds, a regular army is built to destroy with its weapons. God's army uses its weapons to build up. When the church uses spiritual weapons correctly, it builds others up and then God destroys the works of the enemy. Did you catch that? It is God who destroys the works of the enemy. This only happens if we submit, pull out our spiritual artillery, and then hand it over to God. If we make any attempt to do it on our own, we will fail. We will be overcome. And we will be destroyed.

I mention this because we are never out of the sight of Satan's artillery. We may go through periods when everything seems to be going fine, but the truth is that Satan is always on the warpath. Things may be going well, but if we are not in tune with the will of God, we may be heading into a trap of the enemy. It may be a very simple word of deceit that throws us off guard and off course. If we take a look at Eve and her conversation with the serpent we can get a clue of his subtleness. We find this in Genesis 3. The serpent first asked, "Did God say that you shall not eat of every tree in the garden?" Now Eve answered correctly when she said that they could eat the fruit of every tree but the one on the middle of the garden. She also repeated God's command and said that if they ate of this tree, they would die. In verse 4, the serpent told Eve, "You will not die. God does not want you to eat this fruit because your eyes will be opened, you will be like gods and you will know what is good and evil."

The serpent did know the truth and told her only enough of it to make his words sound plausible. He knew that the only way to break ground into the soul of man was to get in there with partial truth. He had to devise a way to get Adam and Eve to sell their birthright and stake claim on the souls of all men and women. After we allow him to take root, he will do anything and everything he can devise to divide the body of Christ. All too often we don't even know that we are being used to divide the body. We follow an idea that sounds scriptural, without checking the Word and the Holy Spirit, and before we know it we have been duped. Trust me, I have played the fool far too many times to count. I have been used by the enemy to cause division in the church before. It was never to the point of a church split, but, nonetheless, it was disruptive to the working of the body. After the dust settled, I wondered how I could have been used to cause such a mess. It was a very uncomfortable feeling to know that I had been so easily led by the wrong spirit. I do not want to go there ever again.

We must remember that God is a unifier and a multiplier and Satan is a divider. God desires us to fulfill His promises on this earth. Satan desires to only destroy the hearts and souls of men and women. He does not want unity to operate in the body of Christ. So, when we hear a word, we have to rightly divide that word. We have to judge whether it is from God or from our enemy. First John 4:1-3 states:

> Beloved, do not believe every spirit, but test the spirits, whether they are of God; because many false prophets have gone out into the world. By this you know the Spirit of God: Every spirit that confesses that Jesus Christ has come in

the flesh is of God, and every spirit that does not confess that Jesus Christ has come in the flesh is not of God. And this is the spirit of the Antichrist, which you have heard was coming, and is now already in the world.

My friends, God asks you to check every word that is claimed to be the word of God. If that word edifies the body, it doesn't necessarily mean that it came from God. If that word confesses that Jesus Christ is Lord and builds up the body, it is from God. We don't have to get into an attitude of "Trust No One," but we should always be careful not to get complacent about what we allow into our soul. You should even check out what I write. As much as I want to glorify God with every word that I type, I am apt to make mistakes.

There is an easy formula to follow when checking what people say is the word from the Lord. Let's go to Galatians 5:19-21:

> Now the works of the flesh are evident, which are: adultery, fornication, uncleanness, lewdness, idolatry, sorcery, hatred, contentions, jealousies, outbursts of wrath, selfish ambitions, dissensions, heresies, envy, murders, drunkenness, revelries, and the like....

If we see any of this in the one delivering the word, we must beware, for they are operating in the works of the flesh and not the Holy Spirit.

The Word of God is very clear about what the enemy uses to bring division in the body of Christ. God is also explicit that those who practice the works of the flesh, as listed above, will not inherit the kingdom of God.

In Galatians 5:22, God tells us how His Spirit operates. "But the fruit of the Spirit is love, joy, peace, long-suffering, kindness, goodness, faithfulness, gentleness, self-control..." The fruit of the Spirit are nine of our weapons of warfare that He uses through us to build up the body of Christ. There is no law to fulfill when operating with the fruit of the Spirit, for they follow the law of love as written in 1 Corinthians 13: 4-8.

> Love suffers long and is kind; love does not envy; love does not parade itself, is not puffed up; does not behave rudely, does not seek its own, is not provoked, thinks no evil; does not rejoice in iniquity, but rejoices in the truth; bears all things, believes all things, hopes all things, endures all things. Love never fails....

You see, we must not only hear what someone is saying, but also how they are saying it. We have to always be on guard to discern the spirit with which a word is given. When we understand the spirit that is leading the individual, we will only war against the wrong spirit and not the individual. Second Corinthians 10:3 says, "For though we walk in the flesh, we do not war according to the flesh."

There is no room for jealousy in the body of Christ. We are called to esteem others more than ourselves. If we desire to operate in the gifts of the Holy Spirit, we must first operate in the love of the Holy Spirit.

The first thing that we wrestle with is our imagination. Most of the time, it is our imagination that gets the best of us. There are also times when we are wrestling with the imaginations of other people. Imagination can easily drive a wedge between two people, or even a group of people, because one person has a thought contrived from only a partial truth. If that person would seek God's face, and ask for His divine guidance on how to handle this situation, the perceived problem would likely end as a simple misunderstanding.

However, most of us tend to ride these vain imaginations for all they are worth. We allow our feelings to get hurt and leave openings for the enemy to activate envy, strife, or jealousy. All of which are the works of the flesh.

If we happen to get caught in the middle of the strife, we need to take a look at the fruit that is being grown. We have to decide whether or not we are going to eat the good fruit or the bad fruit.

Let us step back into the garden of Eden. God told Adam and Eve that they could eat of the fruit of every tree but the tree in the midst of the garden. If they ate of that tree, He said that they would die. Now allow me to go out on a limb for a minute. God gave Adam and Eve trees that gave good fruit. If they ate of those trees, they operated in love, joy, peace, longsuffering, gentleness, goodness, faith, meekness, and temperance. This fruit was scattered throughout the garden and available at all times.

The one tree that they could not eat bore the bad fruit of adultery, fornication, uncleanness, lewdness, idolatry, sorcery, hatred, contentions, jealousies, outbursts of wrath, selfish ambitions, dissensions, heresies, envy, murders, drunkenness, revelries, and the like. One tree with a mixed bag of bad fruit compared to a multitude of trees with luscious and delicious fruit.

If we eat from the tree in the middle of the garden, it will surely cause death. It may not be an immediate, physical death, but the spiritual death is eternal. That is, if someone does not repent and give his heart to Jesus Christ.

The second thing that we battle against is the thing that exalts itself against the knowledge of God. If a word is brought that contradicts God's Word, it is most certainly not from God. We have to rightly divide every word. We have to know and understand God's Word. We have to discern the difference between messages that are like eating candy where there are no wrongs and everything is always good, and a word that edifies and builds us up. Not every word from God will make us feel good or cause goose bumps, but it will always build us up. God may have to give a word that is strong and hard to take, but He will always build us up in the process. He does have to tear down the strong holds that keep us from fulfilling His call on our lives, but during the process He builds us up. He builds us up into the image of His Son, Jesus Christ.

The third thing that we have to do is bring every thought into captivity to the obedience of Christ. As I said earlier, Satan is very subtle and will feed us different thoughts that cause us to question God's Word. These thoughts will tell us that a specific word from

God wasn't real because it has not come to pass. These thoughts will tell us that a brother or sister in Christ did something to offend us. They will tell us that we should skip church because we are mad at someone and they might be there. My friends, these thoughts have to be put into captivity to the obedience of Christ. These thoughts cause division in the body of Christ. Remember, God is a unifier and a multiplier.

The last thing we need to do is to be ready to punish all disobedience when our obedience is fulfilled. This is not saying that we can punish the disobedience of others. When our obedience is fulfilled, we have to punish the disobedience within ourselves. We need to bind up and put into the subjection of Christ those things that influence us into being disobedient. You don't have to make yourself sit in a time-out chair, stand in a corner, or give yourself a whipping. If you have something that enables your disobedience, get rid of it. Disable the opportunity for your flesh to be disobedient to the Lord by removing the thing that it lusts after. Give the Holy Spirit the opportunity to minister to your flesh.

We cannot do these things without using the arsenal of weapons that God has given to us. We have been given weapons for our warfare to overcome vain imaginations, everything that exalts itself above the One True God, the thoughts that try to make us captive, and our disobedience. We now have a list of this arsenal that God uses to help us overcome the attacks of the enemy. Pray for wisdom. Pray for revelation. Attain the victory. And finally, help others win their battles. 2 Cor. 10:4–The weapons of our warfare are not carnal, but mighty through God to the pulling down of strongholds. They are: The word of God, the name of Jesus, obedience, faith, love, forgiveness, prayer, fasting, praise, worship, testimony, humility, joy, peace, long-suffering, gentleness, goodness, meekness, temperance, fear (of the Lord), confession, thankfulness and unity. In Jesus' name, the victory is ours.

DO YOU KNOW JESUS?

> For God so loved the world that He gave His only begotten Son, that whoever believes in Him should not perish but have everlasting life. For God did not send His Son into the world to condemn the world, but that the world through Him might be saved.
>
> John 3:16-17

Since the fall of Adam and Eve in the garden of Eden we have been in a displaced relationship with God. We were created to dwell in fellowship with Him, but our sins placed a barrier between us and God. Man has attempted to bridge that gap through many forms of religion and good works, but the fact remains that we cannot build a bridge over this gulf created by Adam and Eve. In God's infinite love and mercy, He sent His only Son, Jesus, to pay the penalty of sin and forever bridge this gap. It is through His love that sin is forgiven. The only thing that we can do is repent of our sins and ask God to forgive us through the sacrifice of Jesus. Romans 10:9-10 says, that if we confess with our mouth, the Lord Jesus, and believe in our heart that God raised Him from the dead, we shall be saved. For with the heart, man believes, and with the mouth confession is made unto salvation. You may be thinking that you have done too much wrong to be worthy of God's grace. The point is—God loves you!

You are worthy of salvation because Jesus already paid the price for your sins. You can't do anything more or less to make God love you any more than He already does. He desires to have an intimate relationship with you because *you matter to him*!

Please pray this prayer with me: Jesus I love you and I know I am a sinner. I have sinned against you and I am sorry. I believe in you and want you in my life right now. Change my life and take away anything unholy. Help me through each day and to seek you in everything. Teach me to pray, give me the desire to read the Bible and place me into a church. I can't do it myself; only with you can I make it. Help me, Jesus. I praise your name. Put joy in my heart and mouth. Thank you, Jesus. I love you. Amen.